W9-AXS-324

Thanks for supporting this project.
Best,
TAB '08
Pass the word!

CROOKED ROAD STRAIGHT

The Awakening of AIDS Activist Linda Jordan

TINA A. BROWN

"Crooked Road Straight: The Awakening of AIDS Activist Linda Jordan"

Published by TAB Brown Publishing
P.O. Box 567, Hartford, CT. 06141-0567.
(888) 256-1158. First edition.

Copyright © 2008 by Tina A. Brown
All rights reserved. No part of this work shall be reproduced, transmitted, or stored in any form whatsoever, printed or electronic means including information storage and retrieval systems without prior written permission from the publisher, except by a reviewer, who may quote brief passages in a review. Proceeds from this book and associated projects will be used to support HIV/AIDS education.

View www.crookedroadstraight.com and www.tabbrownpublishing.com for more information.

Cover Design by Joseph Hilliman, photograph by Jack McConnell
Book design by Joseph Hilliman
Edited by Kent A. Miles, Rashida Rawls and Susan Schoenberger
Book jacket photograph by Chion Wolf

TAB Brown Publishing
PO Box 567
Hartford, CT 06141
Printed in the United States of America

ISBN: 978-0-9799659-0-6

1. AIDS 2.HIV 3.Heroin 4. Abuse 5.Drugs 6.Childhood 7.Addiction. 8.Redemption 9:Hartford
Inside photographs courtesy of the Jordan, Shannon and Hartie families, and Jack McConnell

Excerpts from the Scripture drawn from the New King James Bible.

DEDICATION

This book of literary nonfiction is dedicated to my God
for teaching me to listen to the Holy Spirit.

Thanks to the late Linda C. Jordan and her family for
generously sharing their stories and opening up their
public records to me. I wrote this book in the hope that
it might change and save the lives of families coping
with drug addiction and learning to live with HIV/AIDS.

CONTENTS

ACKNOWLEDGEMENTS

I THANK GOD first for giving me the courage to see this book to completion. Then, there are Linda Jordan's survivors, Tasha, Samantha and Nicole Jordan; the Shannon family; and Harry Hartie, who believed in this book because it was Linda's wish to have all aspects of her story told.

I thank my friends who helped me: Traci Marquis, Kyra Cross, Lisa Nkonoki, Yolanda Allen, Keith Darby, Trish Willingham, Jackie Peters and Marshann Williams, Wayne Dawkins and Trevy A. McDonald. Thanks to Mrs. Elsie Cofield of the AIDS Interfaith Network Inc. in New Haven, Femi Bogle-Assegai, Gloria Austin, Gladys Pennington, Claudia Rankin, George Sutherland, Debbie Gosselin, Buster Jenkins, Mark Little, Gwendolyn Lewis, Sister Peg, Darrell Decker, Jack McConnell and Father Jerome Massemeno, who were pioneers in the AIDS prevention movement in Connecticut. Thanks also to the Connecticut Department of Children and Families, the Hartford Police Department and so many others who gave me encouragement along the way.

I'm thankful to my mother the Rev. Dr. Cecelia Williams who pushed me to continue writing and to my late father The Rev. Deforest Brown Jr. for teaching me to follow my heart and to tell the stories of our people. I'm especially grateful to Marilyn Strong for giving me a quiet place to write on the Connecticut River. Thanks to the Webb family and others who offered amazing support.

My editing and design team, Kent Miles, Rashida Rawls,

Susan Schoenberger and Joseph Hilliman, showed me that my work is valued. They helped me to make a project into a book. I am also especially grateful to The Hartford Courant, my employer, who gave me opportunities to see and to learn about the city of Hartford.

Also, thanks to my mentors at the National Association of Black Journalists, the organizers of the Nieman and Wesleyan writers workshops; my new partners at AIDS and substance abuse treatment centers, churches and other interested groups.

There were so many others who expressed their well wishes and those I have yet to meet. I am grateful to you all for supporting this book and for putting it into the hands of those who will benefit from it.

"Every valley shall be exalted, and every
mountain and hill shall be made low,
and the crooked shall be made straight
and the rough places plain."

... ISAIAH 40:4

PROLOGUE

AIDS DIDN'T BECOME IMPORTANT to me until somebody I knew died.

I imagine that is also the case for most people in the U.S. Even now, it is easy for most of us to put our thoughts about HIV/AIDS behind us because of the way the disease was introduced into our society. We were told in the mid-1980s that it was an infectious disease killing gay white men, Haitians and intravenous drug users. I didn't know anyone who fit those categories. I had read in school about epidemics throughout history and I never expected to experience this sort of pandemic in my lifetime in such a personal way.

I was a rookie reporter when I heard about AIDS for the first time. The TV broadcaster described it as a mysterious disease that was taking the lives of mostly white gay men in New York and San Francisco. The news report sparked my curiosity. But I didn't think much else about how AIDS would affect me personally until 1986, when one of my colleagues at the Macon Telegraph in Georgia died suddenly.

I was just getting to know this quiet, smart and young black man who worked as a copy editor. Now, he was dead. Though I had volunteered, I hated writing his obituary. I knew so little about this guy's personal life. The word AIDS never appeared in his news obituary. As far as the public was concerned, my colleague died of a sudden illness, a popular buzz phrase coined when young people, mostly men, died of complications related to AIDS or the human immunodeficiency virus that causes the disease. The funeral home directors whispered AIDS as the cause of death for very few people.

His death was unsettling. It became apparent to me that this disease would not just strike white gay men in their prime. I realized that AIDS might become a silent killer in Black America. But there was very little visual evidence of HIV/AIDS affecting this part of the population, despite the statistics made available by the U.S. Centers for Disease Control and Prevention in Atlanta in the mid-1980s. I pushed my concern into the back of my mind.

By 1988 I was trying to advance my career as one of seven journalists selected to go to California to develop my skills at the Summer Program of Minority Journalists — now The Maynard Institute — at the University of California at Berkeley. I was assigned to write about the return of the AIDS Memorial Quilt to the Castro district in San Francisco, at the time the epicenter of the AIDS movement in the U.S. The event was one of the most emotional stories I had written. The quilt had traveled across the U.S. and was displayed at the Capitol in Washington, D.C., before arriving in San Francisco. The mayor of San Francisco and other public officials cried as the thousands of quilt panels were unfolded for miles down a city street.

This disease was real, I thought. I had never seen so many people so emotionally affected by one event. Yet as I looked closer at the quilts being paraded down the street, I noticed that there were very few photographs on display of black faces, particularly of women.

I was touched and felt sympathetic for those affected by

AIDS, but I felt safe as a heterosexual black woman. My feelings about my personal safety changed five years later when the CDC announced that heterosexual black women would be the next wave of people infected by the virus in the Northeast U.S. I fit that demographic. I wondered quietly whether I could become one of those statistics.

That feeling stayed with me when I left my reporting job at the Asbury Park Press in New Jersey for a new reporting position in Hartford, Conn. I promised myself once I got settled that I would write a story about how the black community was responding to HIV/AIDS in Connecticut, especially since so many people in Hartford were infected. I asked my editors: What were the traditional black institutions, especially the churches, doing to help people cope with the disease?

I set out to do that story in 1994. Though in my early 30s, I was naive. My knowledge of the streets and issues associated with poverty were limited. I didn't grow up in the slums. I had never interviewed sex workers or intravenous drug users, people health officials said were also spreading the virus. I admit now that those people scared me because I had seen too many movies.

As the daughter of African Methodist Episcopal ministers, I took the safe approach to the story and called church leaders in cities that dotted Connecticut. To my dismay, they did not return my calls. Since I was working on the special assignment, I didn't have time to wait by the telephone. I ventured out into community-based organizations such as the Urban League and health departments in Hartford, New Britain, New Haven and

Bridgeport to talk to the professionals who were serving the "at risk" populations.

Within a month, I was walking the streets or getting connected with outreach workers like Buster Jenkins and Mark Little in Hartford. Two church mothers, Gladys Pennington and Elsie Cofield, helped direct my path through New Britain and New Haven. They connected me with black and Latino women who told me their life stories, but were unwilling to allow me to use their full names or to have their faces photographed for a newspaper story. Having the virus was a secret many of them kept from their families; they didn't want to reveal their HIV status in The Hartford Courant. So many of them and the outreach workers who distributed condoms, clean needles and bleach kits saw my frustration, and they asked me if I had met Linda Jordan, who was quickly becoming an icon in AIDS prevention communities across Connecticut.

I called Linda and she invited me over to her house in West Hartford, a suburb of Hartford. My first interview lasted about five hours. She told me that she was a recovering heroin addict who was volunteering with seven different AIDS organizations in Connecticut. That work earned her the Mary Fisher Foundation's National Outstanding Caregiver Award in 1993. Linda showed me the posters that she and her daughters and grandson had taken for a public awareness campaign for the Connecticut Department of Revenue and the Concerned Citizens for Humanity. Her family is believed to be one of the first African-American families in the U.S. to put a human face on the disease. The posters are still circulating the globe.

Linda was so open about her story that it struck me as odd that this woman who had experienced a lifetime of tragedies wasn't keeping it a secret. She didn't believe in having skeletons. She shared her HIV status and the status of her oldest daughter, Tanya, and Linda's husband Alvin, who was in prison at the time. I wasn't prepared to hear all of what she had to share in 1994.

My limited street smarts were obvious. It showed in my facial expressions; Linda laughed about it when we talked years later. Yet she trusted that I could learn enough to write her story. At the time, I was too far removed from the life she had led to understand her resilience. She had been molested, abused and raped before she was 10 years old. She had used heroin by the time she was 18, had married and divorced her childhood sweetheart twice. She stayed with him and bore his children, even though he was incarcerated for most of their relationship. She allowed me to hang around, attend family functions and speaking engagements so that I could learn more.

My story for the Courant, "Fighting AIDS with Resilience: Sense of Unity Blacks Confront Epidemic," captured only small fragments of Linda Jordan's life story. I felt unfulfilled after it was published in October 1994 and I went back to my regular beat covering a predominantly white upper middle-class community outside of Hartford.

About six months after the story was published, I was in Puerto Rico for vacation. The ocean has always been a place for clarity for me. I remember sitting on a rock on a beach one day. I felt like I had made the wrong decision by moving to Connecticut. I asked God why he had sent me here. What was I supposed to do in Hartford? I left there thinking that once I returned to Hartford, I had to continue my work reporting about Linda Jordan. I owed her much more as a journalist.

I want to write your book, I told her over the telephone.

When do we start? she responded.

For the next five years, I went to Linda's house on Maplewood Avenue in West Hartford regularly before I went to work at The Courant. I'm not a morning person, so she made sure that I had coffee and she drank tea. I also brought her my copy of the daily newspaper, and was struck that she was always most interested in the obituary page. She recounted the people that she knew had died of AIDS, had overdosed on heroin or died of other premature deaths because of their lifestyles.

My concern back in the early 1980s that black American women would have to wake up and respond to this disease became clear and present. Like in the early days, very few if any of the obituaries cited the true causes of death when someone died of AIDS. So many people were dying in secret and ashamed. But here I was sitting at Linda Jordan's kitchen table amazed that she didn't look sick. She was very much alive. She was not afraid to reveal her HIV status and the diagnosis of her husband and her oldest daughter. She strongly believed if those in the HIV/AIDS community stopped hiding their status, more people would accept that the disease was claiming so many others and leaving their families to cope in secret. She told her story to anyone who would listen, hoping and praying that it would be the catalyst for other women who had gone down her crooked path to change their lifestyles.

Over time, my assignment at The Courant changed. In 1998, I started writing about crime, courts and social trends in Hartford, one of the poorest cities in the nation. My time in Hartford was not wasted as I became able to write Linda's story with authority. I was here to see the housing projects where Linda grew up before the federal government tore them down. I witnessed the impact of the AIDS epidemic among the intravenous drug community in this city and others. I saw how welfare reform changed the life of a third-generation welfare recipient who moved into the world of work not just as an AIDS outreach worker, but as a factory worker once the monthly stipends she received for most of her life dried up.

Linda's story is about living with AIDS. Her spiritual development and belief in God once she forced her way into drug treatment taught her that she could live without the medications that so many people depend upon today. Her unfilled wish was that all religious leaders, especially those in the black church, would stand and help those with the virus who were lost and forgotten. She believed that God saved her from killing herself and AIDS was just something she had to live with. She used her life story to show others that change is possible.

This story affirmed my reasons for becoming a journalist 23 years ago. I chose this profession to tell stories about the people in our society who are largely ignored by the general public. Fortunately, my mission has placed me in unfamiliar situations and enabled me to grow up and reach inside myself to find a common ground with most of the people I've interviewed.

"Crooked Road Straight: The Awakening of AIDS Activist Linda Jordan" was written so that people of all races, ages, class and generations could reflect on their lives, their past sins and troubles and come to grips with things that hurt them. Linda had to forgive a lot of people because she knew that God had forgiven her. Hers is a story about choosing life despite the odds.

There are a lot of lessons to be learned from Linda's story. She accepted the roots of her pain that led to her addictions. Once she accepted her faults, she learned to live.

This book is a dream come true for both of us.

CHAPTER 1 | DEMONS

SWEAT DRIPPED FROM LINDA'S FOREHEAD as she cupped her bony knees in a corner of the city-issued cot. The thin sheets, musty with her sweat, produced a smell that sucked the fresh air from the tiny cubicle-size room at the Blue Hills Treatment Center in Hartford, Conn. Her nostrils burned and her stomach ached.

Linda stayed like that, rocking herself until a chill swept through her emaciated body. The cold was a new sensation. It replaced the drug-induced warmth that had kept her company for the twenty years she mainlined dope into the veins of her arms and into her toes. A new stage of her detoxification was beginning. But the demons of the addiction that had stolen her identity up to this point were wrestling for a permanent place in her thirty-eight year-old mind. For now, Linda was winning. She shut out her cravings, closed her eyes and prayed. The stomach cramps that had doubled her over with pain during the first five days suddenly stopped. A mental light bulb came on as she pulled the hospital gown over her exposed buttocks, curled her body into an "s" and drifted off into a faraway place not yet forgotten.

Suddenly, visions of her past went through her mind inside the locked ward of the treatment center. In her visions, she was a toddler running through the tobacco and corn fields near the Massachusetts border. In her daydream, Linda fancied being back on the farm. She felt as if she were on another planet, different from the concrete sidewalks where weeds burst through the cracks. She loved it out there the very first time she jumped off Granddaddy's truck.

In her reminiscence, she was awed by the vastness of the land, the absence of tall buildings, potholes and crowded tenements of Hartford. Nobody stopped her that first time Linda took off running into the fields, right out of her shoes. She ran until her skinny legs collapsed like pretzels, giving her time to squeeze the mushy dirt between her toes. The warmth of the muddy soil felt like chocolate pudding, and she giggled.

While basking in the sun, Linda picked up a giant tobacco leaf she found in the fields. She waved it in her hand like one of the fans she often found tucked between Bibles in her Grandma's church. The leaf felt like boot leather, tough as Mommy's belt.

Linda was a child of the ghetto, the product of a landscape of concrete. In the country, when the adults weren't watching, she felt like she was a dancing princess. In the distance, she gazed into the sunlight and saw stalks heavy with New England sweet and butter corn. She ran until she reached the rows of corn neatly positioned in long straight lines.

"Sweets," she mouthed.

She reached up to grab a stalk but her skinny legs weren't long enough. She jumped and tried to climb before settling on an ear she found in the dirt. The sun burnt cob had the sweetness of a baby's pacifier, reminding Linda of Kool-Aid and candy canes, her childhood favorite treats. She peeled the husk and ate one cob and then another, dropping the last ear into the sandy dirt, and burying it with her bare feet. The corn gave rise to a burst of energy. She ran, leaped and galloped with the vigor she had playing hopscotch and double-dutch on the sidewalks of a housing project near her home.

Running emancipated Linda, a descendant of grandparents with country Southern roots. Out here, she was free to roam away from the confusing rants of raging drunks, crying babies and fights over toys with her siblings.

The sounds of crickets and frogs in the nearby creek helped her to acknowledge that she was just a little girl, too young to milk a cow or to pluck a chicken. She was left alone in the fields until the sun glowed orange just before the darkness fell and the moon displayed its own light.

Even at the tender age of three, Linda knew the consequences for staying outside past dark. The joy of playing in dirt, the sweet nectar of the corn and the toughest of the tobacco leaves would be traded for a whipping with a hickory switch or a strong leather belt if she failed to come in by sundown.

She made it back in time to the farmhouse where the sharecroppers lived and looked forward to repeating the ritual every bright day that first day of summer from daybreak to dawn. Nothing disturbed the joy and merriment she felt on the farm until the day the clouds turned dark as Granddaddy rode up behind her on his mule-drawn buggy, while she was leaning over a creek looking for fish.

"You wanna ride?"

The memory of the sound of Granddaddy's voice, deep, husky and Southern, cracked open a tortured place inside her mind. His voice ripped at her insides like a heroin jones. It made her body jerk repeatedly with convulsions, causing her to hit the emergency button on the edge of her cot.

The buzzer sounded an alarm for a duty nurse, who ran to assist her. The gray-haired lady, whose face concealed her age, found Linda kicking and wailing for mercy at the edge of the cot. Guessing that Linda was fighting off a craving for heroin, Linda's personal Mary Seacole, the famous 19th century West Indian nurse, consoled her.

"Don't worry Linda this too shall pass," the nurse whispered. "This too shall pass."

The woman in the starched white dress and matching cap was only about five feet tall, but had muscular and sturdy arms and legs. She lifted Linda's limp bare naked body off the cot as both of them caught a whiff of the disgusting scents from the bedpan.

"Oooh, you've been busy," the nurse joked, hoping to jolt Linda out of her mental malaise.

Linda was incapable of responding. Her mind remained fixed on the dream that was revealing itself as the sound of her Granddaddy's voice. She hadn't heard his voice since she was five years old. Nothing now, not even the aches and pains of her heroin withdrawal, could block the sound of his voice and visions of her days in the fields. She no longer had to close her eyes to see the corn, the tobacco leaves and the creek.

"It whatn't no dream," Linda cried aloud as she rested her face against the cold concrete wall.

"Whatcha say?" the nurse asked.

"It wasn't no dream," Linda said, her voice so loud that it echoed against the concrete walls.

The nurse was familiar with the revelations her patients had as their bodies and minds freed themselves of an intoxicating drug. She busied herself with the bedpan and left Linda to the thoughts enveloping her conscious mind.

Linda didn't notice when the nurse exited the room. Her mind stayed fixed on what came next in the picture show projecting in her mind. She saw Granddaddy's scrawny brown face, tattooed with razor cuts and flaunting a toothless grin. The odor of the sweat on his tobacco-stained hands filled her nose while tears burned down her cheeks. Though she was a grown woman, Linda sucked on her index and middle fingers, a habit she had developed as a toddler. It pacified Linda as she curled closer to the edge of the cot. She saw herself on Granddaddy's lap as he rode a buggy guided by a bowlegged mule. Its hoofs left tracks throughout the fields.

Throughout the bumpy ride, Granddaddy clinched his thick arms around Linda's waist with the tightness of a seat belt, making her initially feel safe. The buggy's height made it easier for Linda to see the blazing sun, the mushy dirt, the leathery leaves and the stalks of sweet corn from up high. Granddaddy disturbed her concentration once he moved one of his thick hands between her thighs, making her wiggle and twist. He tightened his grip on her bony long fingers, steering them closer to the private part of his overalls during the rest of the journey.

"Stroke it baby," he whispered. "That's a good gal."

Linda tilted her head up and noticed that Granddaddy's toothless smile showed pleasure as he tightly gripped her inner thighs. She felt funny about what he was doing and it made her stomach queasy. She yelled out for him to stop, but he held on tighter. She hoped that the sound of panic in her voice would make him release his thick black fingers. But it didn't. Linda squeezed her eyes shut and sucked her fingers when the mule tired just outside the barn. She opened her eyes as Granddaddy released his grip.

Grandma was standing beside the buggy, holding a hose and a bucket filled with soapy water.

"Com' on here gal. Where you been all day?"

Linda smiled at being rescued. She leaped out of Granddaddy's lap onto a dirt pile.

"Is you a boy? Or a gal?" Grandma asked sarcastically.

"I's a gal," Linda answered as Grandma hosed off the dirt covering Linda's feet and hands, washing away all the dirty feelings that had collected in her young mind during the bumpy ride. The sun was going down.

Linda pushed back those thoughts and fixated on the smells of fried chicken and sweet potato pie breezing from inside the sharecroppers' cabins. The confusion that she'd felt about what Granddaddy did drifted back into her memory.

For the next few days, Granddaddy let her run and play and had reverted back to his introverted ways. Linda took off running again into the fields. But now she looked over her shoulder. She listened closely for sounds of the mule hooves and planned to hide under the rows of the corn if she heard Granddaddy approaching her sanctuary.

She felt safe again, until the day she wandered into the wooden barn to pick with her favorite cow. She stood on the three-legged stool next to the old worn-out heifer, preparing to touch its furry back, when she felt Granddaddy push up behind her. She could tell he was in one of his sour and touchy moods.

"Time you sucked it," Granddaddy said, undoing his denim trousers so his privates peeked out. "Suck it, ya' here? Suck it now!"

Linda's tiny body shook as she leaped off the stool, hoping to run faster than the old man. He was quicker and he snatched her bony hand and yanked her back into the barn. Granddaddy's contorted expression scared Linda so much that she screamed until the back of her throat hurt. The sound of her panic this time threw off Granddaddy long enough for her to wrestle her way past the cow, the horses and chickens, and out of the barn. When he caught up with her, his look was square and threatening as he picked up a horse's bridle lying on the ground.

"I ain't done nothing!" Linda yelled, expecting a beating.

She didn't get a chance to say any more before he clamped her mouth shut with his oversized hand that felt like a leather strip. Linda passed out right there in the barn and daydreamed that she was running against the horror, so far and long into the fields that nobody would find her.

Granddaddy went for the bait, and before he knew it, Linda

was up on her feet. She ran this time until sweat dripped off her forehead like an outdoor spigot. She raced away from the nightmare, back into the corn in the fields, the tobacco leaves and the dirt she mashed between her toes near the creek.

After the second time, Linda was afraid of Granddaddy. She let out an unruly shrill each time she saw him headed her way. If he came through the front door, she screamed. If he was in the kitchen when she drifted in for breakfast, she screamed. Grandma and Mommy thought Linda had lost her mind, and every time she yelled, they gave her something to "cry 'bout."

Granddaddy stopped his fingering and sucking game the day he died. Linda was five years old. Now, more than thirty years later, Linda jerked herself back up in the cot and sobbed as she pieced together her memory of the incident. She remembered the scent of Granddaddy's tobacco juice-stained hands. The thought of it made her nauseous. She felt the same urge to run as she had when she was a child. She ran past the bedpan out of the nasty-smelling room and into the treatment center's community bathroom, where she vomited so violently that her ribs ached. Once she got the strength to get up from the cold tiles on the floor, Linda looked into the mirror and splashed water on her face, hoping to calm her nerves before she returned to her room and crawled back onto her cot. She forced her eyes to stay open until sunlight pushed through the mini-blinds.

Finally, the midnight blues brought on by a succession of nightmares that mirrored her life made sense. Now, other memories that had faded in her heroin-induced haze became crystal clear.

CHAPTER 2 | THE SPERIMENT

LINDA'S MIND TOOK HER BACK to the point when getting high became an irresistible temptation. It was way past midnight on one of those nights that Linda felt squeezed too tightly on life's rocky roads, when she finally laid down and rolled over into a wet spot on one of the twin beds she shared with her three sisters.

"Damn," she said, sitting up and resting her elbows against her knees. "Somebody peed."

She was only 18 and her life was already spinning out of control.

She looked around in the night sky and felt only darkness inside as she sucked her two fingers like a pacifier.

"I gotta get out of Hartford."

The crack between the twin beds was the only dry place to sleep. She sat there and tried to calm her restless mind. Earlier in the night, Linda got between Mommy and Daddy King, and she felt the distress of her stupidity now as she rubbed her thick swollen lips.

"Ax-cident. It was an Ax-cident," Mommy slurred to the policeman who banged on the door of her family's North Main

Street apartment to investigate the disturbance.

"Is that really what happened?" the burly white cop asked.

"Yeah."

Lying to the cop that night saved both Mommy and Daddy King from being arrested. But Linda knew when the sun rose there would be no hiding from the social worker who had heard about the fight from neighbors. Like always, the bookish-looking woman would threaten to take away the family's food stamps and the family's checks from The Welfare if the police were called again.

Linda was restless. She stared outside into the full moon and felt as damned as any young black teenager struggling to survive in impossible circumstances.

"I always get in the middle of they shit," she told herself. She always was the one to end up with a bloody lip, a hurt behind and a cracked psyche.

"Why me? Why not somebody else in this damn family? I'm goin' do something to satisfy me. Me. Just me," she said as she dried her eyes, vowing that "something" was about to change.

Linda made a pact with herself that today was the day of the speriment, a dare that she and her best friend Vee had talked about. She continued her day as usual and didn't say anything to anyone about her plans. As she washed the breakfast dishes, wiped the kitchen table and cleaned the bacon grease from the stove, Linda contemplated a perfect time to go down into the basement with her friend Vee.

"Time me and Vee stop playing and do the damn thang. Okay!" she lectured to herself as she scrubbed the walls and baseboards. She waited until everybody was out of the house except for Mommy. Linda did everything expected of a teenager with grown up responsibilities like herself. She washed out the face bowl, the tub, the toilet, and scrubbed the kitchen floor on her hands and knees before Mommy's afternoon stories came on the living room TV set. Mommy would be liquored up by mid-day and Linda could get on with her plans.

A sense of satisfaction overwhelmed her. She was glad that she lived in a family where nobody raised concerns about how she acted until she did something so crazy, like the times she ran away or took too many pills the doctor gave her when she was twelve to ease her nerves. Then they were forced to pay attention.

Linda finished her chores and took a seat in Daddy King's cracked leather easy chair next to Mommy, who had drifted off to sleep. She watched "The Price is Right" in peace until the screen on the secondhand black-and-white TV set started acting up. Mommy's stories were starting anyway, Linda told herself as she fiddled with the channel knobs with a screwdriver, hoping to stop the screen from rolling. Today, just like yesterday and probably tomorrow, Mommy was deep into an alcoholic coma.

Linda changed the TV's three channels and adjusted the bunny-ear antenna as quickly as she could, hoping that her movements wouldn't waken Mommy.

The first of the month was always easier for everyone in the family. The postman dropped off their checks and food stamps from The Welfare like Santa Claus delivered toys to rich kids on Christmas morning. There would be food in the house, and

Mommy would have money for liquor, which gave her comfort. Linda refilled the glasses that rested on the water-stained coffee table. Her glass of grape Kool-Aid was so full of sugar that the white crystals settled like sand at the bottom. Mommy had a jelly glass filled with more vodka than juice. She happily slept with a Pall Mall cigarette burning in the ashtray.

Daddy King would be at the front door in a few hours kicking off the dirt from his steel-toe boots, and demanding the supper he expected to be on the table. By then, Linda thought, she would be back upstairs and she would be done with the speriment. Nobody would be the wiser, especially since her older brother and sister were visiting their grandmother.

Linda knew a few things about her parents. They were creatures of habit. While Daddy worked, Mommy drank. When he got home, Daddy tied one on, too. Then they'd take their respective places in a duel over who could scream the loudest before one of them passed out or was knocked out. The maddening dance that Linda's parents called their marriage lacked sweet love songs and wet kisses. Mommy's shrieks and the sounds of broken glass most nights made their five children restless at night and cranky in the mornings. Mommy and Daddy King made life hard for Linda, who carried the load of being a responsible daughter like a slave carried bales of cotton on her back.

Mommy was incapable of playing the role of wifey on days like today. She got her private cocktail party started right after the westerns and game shows, when every good housewife, even in a century-old tenement, was taking a break in front of the TV. This afternoon, Linda watched Mommy all comfy lying slothfully on the plastic-covered sofa. She was tempted to return to her seat beside Mommy to watch the shows she liked, but she stayed committed to her plan.

"I gotta do it now," she said as she raced to the rotary telephone and dialed up Vee's number.

"She on one," Linda whispered. "You still up for the 'speriment?'"

Though she remained silent, Vee was as curious as Linda about getting into something when neither one of them needed to worry about the watchful eye of a discerning parent. Vee was Linda's girl; they'd grown close since elementary school, and even closer since that rainy night years ago when they ran away to an abandoned building they'd affectionately called "their 'partment." The adventure would forever seal their loyalty. Despite the fact that they'd been caught and dragged back home together, neither of them would ever tell their secret about the box of silver dollars they had found in the abandoned building. They shared each other's desires of freedom and secret loves like stolen lipstick and a teenage girl's yearning to escape the blues that always percolated inside the three-story concrete tenement where they lived.

"I'll be here when you get here," Linda said in her regular exasperating way. Her own stomach pinched with cramps; now that she had made the call, it was time to put up or shut up.

She had time to get the syringes ready before Vee arrived.

While Mommy slept, Linda turned on the bathroom faucet full blast so the rust could spit out before the water flowed clear to fill the syringes. She caught herself admiring her Hershey chocolate brown skin in the cracked mirror and had a reassuring talk with herself.

"They call me Blackie and Buckwheat, but I knows I's beautiful," she told herself. She didn't mind Buckwheat because on TV, his character was a movie star on "The Little Rascals."

"I's a star, too, and I'm a gonna reach for the stars today. Okay!" Linda told herself.

The faucet whistled. The sound made her bristle as she thought that at any moment Mommy would stumble up behind her and thump her on the back of her head for wasting water.

"That $50 a month check you get from The Welfare ain't big enough to cover no damn water bill. Turn that shit off!" Mommy had said it so many times that Linda heard it like an eight-track tape inside of her head.

Linda calmed her own nerves as the water slowed, remembering that Mommy was too tanked up with booze to pay attention. Her appetite for vodka and her favorite daytime stories was as big and wide as Linda's love for her boyfriend, beer and cigarettes she found whole in the ashtray.

"This ain't working," Linda scolded herself as a gush of water splashed out of a syringe over the face bowl and onto the floor.

"Shit, shit, shit," she cursed the mess.

Experience taught Linda that she had to clean up her mess. She decided to fill the syringes half way because she would need the rest of her time to sop up the water that collected around the face bowl and on the floor with a rag. Again, Linda imagined the worst. What if Mommy woke up with an uncontrollable urge to pee, barged her way into the bathroom and slipped before cracking her head on the toilet seat? The thought compelled Linda to get on her hands and knees to wipe the floor now soaking the edges of her bell bottoms.

"Linda! You in there?"

"Linda! Linda!" Vee knocked on the bathroom window. "Answer the door!"

"I'm comin', hold yo' horses," Linda called out. "Damn, you scared the shit out of me. I almost slipped and broke my behind."

Linda squeezed the water out of the rag and hung it back on the bucket. She slid the water-filled syringes into a side pants pocket before spying on Mommy in the front room.

"Is she out cold?" Vee whispered as she yanked off her winter cap and took off her overcoat at the back door.

"Yea, I think so. Come on in. You thirsty?"

At the kitchen table Linda and Vee slurped down Kool-Aid from jelly glasses for what seemed like an eternity until Vee stuttered out what Linda was thinking.

"We gon' do it for real?"

"Yeah, gurl, you know I'm game."

"Did you bring the flashlight?"

"You got them things you found?

"I'm straight," Linda answered. "I just want to wait until the first part of Mommy's stories go off. She gotta be good and full before we do anything. Wait here."

Linda bumped into the coffee table, jiggling the ice cubes in Mommy's glass when she reached down for a full inspection.

She worried for a second that she was disturbing Mommy's blissful catnap. No chance. She was lying face down in the bed of the cloth throw pillows covering the sofa. Linda could hear her sucking her teeth.

"I hopes she don't roll over on the floor," Linda mumbled.

Earlier that morning after Linda finished cleaning up, she put chicken backs, necks and onions in a pot on the stove to slow cook. "We'll be back in here tending to the pot before Mommy gets up," Linda said, stopping at the doorway.

She noticed Vee staring into space the way she always did when she was thinking too hard. "Let's do this," Linda said loudly, jolting Vee out of her daze.

They walked slowly to the rear entrance looking suspiciously around the corner for nosy neighbors. The hallway was dark despite the light from a busted window above the back door. They felt under their feet the soggy plaster dampened by dripping water from the exposed overhead pipes.

Linda and Vee tensed as they turned the corner, holding onto the wall to guide their way. They could smell garbage and human waste as their shoes crushed syringes and rat droppings covering the floor in their path. None of this scared Linda as she pulled Vee along by the hand. Her mission was in full throttle. After years of living in this decrepit red-brick building, originally intended to house families temporarily after World War II, Linda and Vee were used to the stench left behind by junkies, hobos and drunks. They didn't even cover their noses, though the smell burned their eyes.

Just as Linda suspected, everybody around was too drunk,

high or fixated on their afternoon soaps to hear her unlatching the basement door. They paused in their sopping wet, dirty sneakers as they waded through the cobwebs at the entrance of the staircase.

"Watch your step," Linda warned as she slid her slim body down one toothless plank after another into the place where the vagrants and rats slept at night. She had been in the basement rambling for cigarette butts the previous summer when she stumbled upon a stash of needles hidden behind some boxes. She knew then that she and Vee would use the basement to conduct the speriment.

The seasons had changed twice since Linda brought up the subject about taking a trip down into the basement. She broached the subject with Vee one evening as she pushed her friend on a swing surrounded by weeds while they watched tall skinny boys nearby playing basketball on the cracked concrete court at the hoop without a net.

"You wanna get high?"

Vee nodded, not knowing exactly whether Linda meant for her to count the pennies that collected in her piggybank to pay for a bottle of cheap wine or for a nickel bag of weed. Linda explained that they would need to practice skin-popping, as Alvin, her boyfriend, had called it.

"If we try the needle with just water inside, it won't hurt," Linda promised. "All we got to do is stick it under the skin. Then, when we get us some real dope, we won't waste it. 'Waste not want not,' " Linda mumbled while pushing Vee on the swing higher and higher until her friend's legs kicked up in flight.

Linda learned that phrase from Mommy on one of the days she was sober enough to teach her how to make soup from left-over chicken parts after the food stamps ran out at the end of the month. "Waste not, want not," Linda repeated.

"Huh?" Vee said, confused by Linda's explanation.

"We'll call it 'the 'speriment'," Linda said, loudly interrupting Vee's daydream of one day making it out of the crappy part of the city they had nicknamed "Hardford."

Neither of them spoke again about "the 'speriment" until months later when they made it down the last of the toothless planks, a poor excuse for a staircase. Linda held the flashlight as Vee screwed in the light bulb. They gazed at the syringes and the pieces of rope they cut from the backyard clothes line. Vee had seen other syringes that dope users littered around the grounds of the nearby housing projects, but unlike Linda, she was too afraid to pick them up.

"You ready?" Linda said as Vee inspected Linda's tiny fore-arms in the light. Linda was always the smallest girl in the neigh-borhood, but her loud mouth made up for her pint size.

"Tie it tight," she demanded.

Vee and Linda were best friends, but Vee was clearly the fol-lower in the pair and responded to Linda's commands as if she was a dutiful soldier. She knew Linda had the courage of a pit bull, ready to pick a fight if challenged. Still, Vee paused as she noticed Linda clenching her teeth in anticipation of the needle prick. She quietly prayed that Linda would change her mind.

"We got to practice. Okay!" Linda commanded.

Fearful of Linda's scorching temper, Vee pulled Linda's arm

closer in the faint light and noticed goose bumps inching up her friend's arm.

"Damn, it's cold down here," Linda said, breaking the silence. "You ready, girl? Don't get scary on me now."

When Vee pricked her friend's skin for the first time, Linda surprised them both as she screamed like a child getting vaccinated at the clinic. "Ouch. Ouch."

Her despair made both of them jump. "Damn, that thing stings," Linda admitted.

She didn't know if it was the coldness of the needle prick, the glare of the flashlight, or the fact that she and Vee were "'sperimenting" in that cold-ass basement that made her body betray her and stiffen up. But she stayed strong as any project warrior, thinking that she would get payback when it was Vee's turn.

Linda averted her almond-shaped eyes from the place where Vee inserted the needle. No matter how many times she hollered, Linda cut her eyes back at Vee.

"They say if you toughen up your muscles, you get used to the pain of it goin' in."

Linda wasn't as afraid of pain. Her legs and arms had already been toughened from years of abuse from tree branches, extension cords, belt straps and words that crushed her heart every time somebody called her "Blackie."

"This ain't shit. I know when we do get the real deal, it's gon' be different," Linda promised.

For a split second, Linda fixed her eyes on the fear she saw in Vee's big brown eyes while shaking off the goose bumps that exposed her own fear. Deep inside she desperately needed to practice, even if Vee didn't.

"They say that dope make you feel all warm inside, you know like the way you feels when somebody cover you up with a thick blanket on a freezing cold night. I be watching. I see how them junkies lie back when they feels the heat. I wanna moan and let go of everything. If it mean taking the pain of the needle, I'm all right with that. Okay," Linda preached.

After one or two tries, Linda had had enough. Tears she hoped Vee wouldn't see were welling up in the corners of her eyes.

"That's good. Okay! Let me do you."

Vee had held back her own tears as long as she could. She wasn't as strong as her friend. Linda knew deep down that Vee was too afraid of the 'speriment to take her turn. Secretly, she was relieved that Vee was too terrified of needles and she didn't press the point, at least this time.

"You'll get over it," Linda said, reassuring her friend that today would not be the day that she would face the prick of an icy cold needle.

"Let's go, girl," Linda yelled as they made it to the top of the stairs.

The basement was the best place for the 'speriment. Nobody went down there in the daytime. If Mommy woke up from her drunken stupor, she would never suspect that Linda was brave enough to go into the cold damp basement to practice with needles. As the two teenage girls waded back through the nasty hallway into the back door, Linda regained her confidence and Vee recoiled inside herself.

"I figured when we finally do cop, I didn't wanna waste none," Linda said softly, trying to ease the tension heating up between them.

"I want it to go smooth and easy," Linda joked.

"You crazy, girl," Vee laughed nervously.

The pressure between them lifted as soon as Vee unscrewed the light bulb with the tail end of her shirt. Linda closed and then latched the back door. About the same time, the pressure cooker on the stove started whistling, sounding an alarm that it was time for them to get back upstairs. Inside the apartment, where the light was better, Vee noticed that rings of sweat had formed under Linda's underarms. Before she could say anything, Linda walked out of the kitchen to check on Mommy.

Like clockwork, the credits were rolling on the TV screen. The show had gone off. Mommy was still dreaming, probably about later that night when she would slip out of bed into the bathroom to get her midnight sip inside a mouthwash bottle. Linda strutted back into the kitchen with the exaggerated sway of a streetwalker. Her confidence even made her voice sound like a character in a bad movie.

"Hell, the pain ain't no worse than Mommy's switch from the tree branch on one of them nights at the end of the month when she burns up my behind for no reason. You know she always get mad when all the cookie jar change left over from the grocery money is gone and she mad cause she ain't got no vodka. I know just how she feels. But that cheap wine I be sneaking don't do the trick for me no more," Linda told Vee. She had hoped the tone of her voice would break the silence and once again seal tight another secret between she and her friend.

Vee stayed deep in thought as she examined the chipped polish on her badly bitten fingernails. Her silence and somber mood made Linda think, too. She knew that no matter how much Vee practiced skin-popping, the water shooting out the works into her own skin had stung like bumble-bees chasing her around the weeds littering the yard on hot summer days.

"Curing the pain is like medicine round here," Linda said. "Seem like everybody round here is gettin' high. Why should we be left out?"

Vee smeared the last of her dime store lipstick on her thick lips with the tip of her finger without a word. The makeup didn't help, though, Linda thought. Her friend had painted on a smile, but she looked tired at the thought of what they had done. She had the face of a spinster who had lived a life of regrets and lost loves.

"Cat got your tongue?" Linda teased sarcastically, as she reached behind Vee and tickled her under her arms.

"Stop. Stop," Vee laughed. "You sooo crazy."

"Next time, you go first," Linda warned as she pinched her friend.

"Now that didn't hurt did it? Com' on girl, you want it too. I see how you be lookin' at them guys resting in the halls after dark lookin' satisfied," Linda said as she turned her back from the sink to wash her hands with the same soap she used to make bubble baths.

"We best friends, right? Right?

"Yeah girl," Vee smiled.

"You ain't goin' fake out on me, is you?"

"Nah," Vee said softly.

"Girl! Please! If Alvin chase that dope like he do them fast girls in mini-skirts it must be good. You know how he likes him some pussy, always did," she said, smiling.

Vee giggled nervously.

"Here I'm the mama of his baby girl, who need baby formula, clothes, diapers and pins and he ain't studyin' us," Linda said as she poured Vee another glass of grape Kool-Aid. " I be thinking he done disappeared with some other girl, and he done raced up to Harlem with some of his older friends to pick up that dope. Oh, I'm gon' to fix his black ass. Okay! I ain't goin' to be left out.

"Now, don't get me wrong. I ain't trying to get hooked or nothin.' I just want a little comfort. Okay!"

CHAPTER 3 | FEELS LIKE FLYING

A FEW WEEKS LATER when they ventured into the basement, Linda had copped a bag of heroin.

Vee went first this time, and she immediately nodded off, leaving Linda to shoot up by herself. After practicing skin popping, Linda felt confident when she removed the jump rope tied around Vee's arm. Her hand shook as she pulled one end of the tattered rope tightly around her own bony arm until she clenched it tight with her teeth and formed a knot. She cooked the dope in a Coke bottle top before injecting it into her arm. A candle was still burning and provided the faint light she needed. There was no use in nudging Vee, now incapable of holding up the flashlight anyway.

"I can do this," Linda told herself. "I can do this."

Linda thought of herself as an experienced skin popper after a dozen times down the basement. But this was the real thing. She was nervous about injecting too much. Nothing prepared her for the sight of her own blood and it overpowered her. She was laid out on the cool cement floor when Vee sat up and looked around for Linda. Vee immediately thought Linda was dead beside her, and she panicked.

"Linda! Linda! Don't die on me. Don't die on me!"

Linda's mind drifted off but she heard Vee's hysterical cries. She kept quiet and listened before opening her eyes. The heat from the dope had filled her body and she wanted to savor it. Vee's crying gave Linda strange reassurance that Vee was her only true best friend. She kept her eyes shut, comforted by that thought. Finally, she couldn't listen to Vee's suffering anymore. She opened her eyes and sprung to her feet.

"What, what?" Linda said, cracking a smile.

"Gurl, you scared the stew out of me. Stop your foolishness," Vee ordered.

The funny thing was Linda didn't feel anything much during the real 'speriment, except for the feeling that an electric blanket had warmed her insides on a frosty night in Hartford. The feeling instantly broke a chill inside as Linda got up and brushed off the dirt that had collected on her new polyester jersey. She vowed she would never need that feeling as much as the junkies on the street and the ones in her family.

"Just for fun, girl," she told Vee. "Nothing serious. Just for fun."

The two of them cuddled together until their highs went down, and they got up and drifted back upstairs.

After a few more times, when they got used to the feeling of the narcotic floating through their veins, the two teenage girls grew courageous. They ventured out of the basement on one of the first spring days when a fresh breeze outside beckoned them. Linda didn't speak until she reached the door. She was determined to spread her arms out, so she could fly like the birds she saw perched on the few tree branches planted outside her family's apartment building. The higher she felt, the more she wanted to show off her new hairdo and the bell bottom pants suit that she had saved for.

"God knows I had to get out of that house," Linda said as she stretched her arms out for flight. "Whee, whee," she yelled.

Vee was aghast. Linda was embarrassing her. She couldn't believe Linda was acting such a fool on North Main Street, a major roadway on the black side of Hartford. She ignored Linda the best she could, but the noise she was making gave Vee a headache.

"Whee, whee," Linda said while trying to hold back her laughter. Old women in the neighborhood pulled back their curtains to watch as Linda passed the corner hot-dog vendor, who stationed his wiener wagon near the Bellevue Square housing project. The older man, who had often chided Linda for acting fast, looked her dead in the eyes as they passed.

"Ain't none of ya'll goin' ruin my thang today," Linda said nonchalantly. "Not even that old wiener man who always be trying to tell me what to do. He ain't my damn daddy."

Linda didn't realize how annoyed Vee was with her drama until she tugged at her from behind. "Stop. Stop, Linda," Vee said. "You ruining' my shit. Now, stop!"

Linda was tripping the way she wanted to, even if her dime-store platforms had stayed planted firmly on the ground. She got louder and she giggled to herself when she saw the church women peek around behind their clotheslines where they often congregated to gossip about the antics of Linda, "that crazy ass Shannon girl."

"Whee, whee," Linda yelled. "I feels like flying."

Vee prayed quietly that none of the responsible adults who stood around the clotheslines or behind the curtains in their windows would phone the police or her momma. She wasn't as high as Linda but she wanted to stay connected to the way she felt, more mellow and woozy and aware that she and her friend were exposing their secret to all of North Main Street.

"Not today! Even you ain't goin' to ruin my high," Linda said, poking Vee in the cheek with an index finger. "Not even you!"

She stretched her arms out like wings and spun around so her bell bottoms flapped, making her feel like she could fly.

A voice swirling inside Linda's head sounded like water gurgling down an unclogged drain. Her brain started spinning and her mind felt like everything had suspended in time. The dope was in control. Linda's head flopped up and down and her chin beat against her chest.

She was crashing.

"I must look real crazy to all them folks peeking out they shades," she thought.

She suddenly caught her balance and was as tired as those dime-store skippies on her feet. "Vee." It came out a whisper.

Linda stood there for a second nodding as in a dream and twisting her feet in the cracks of the sidewalk. She had lost track of time but didn't know for how long. She woke up sitting on the curb with a taste for an orange soda on her lips.

"Um, um," Linda grunted to herself as her head flopped and

her nose ran like she had a mid-season cold. She looked up in time to see Alvin's big red Cadillac skidding up to the curb at her feet.

"Linda! Linda! Get your ass in this damn car!" Alvin yelled. His words cut through Linda's spine like a sharp knife.

"Hey, baabyyy," Linda slurred. "What's up?"

Alvin got out the car and strutted in Linda's direction while Linda collected her thoughts. "Get up! Get up! You gon' tell me what you done had!" Alvin screamed while he shook Linda's shoulders with both hands.

"Nothin'."

Alvin cut his eyes at Vee, but he focused his anger on Linda. His body language showed Vee that he didn't think much of her at that moment.

Alvin had street smarts. He knew immediately what had gone on. He promised himself that he would force Linda to confess. He was concerned about his baby's mama as he yanked Linda up from off the curb like a rag doll.

Vee stood frozen. She wanted to move and to say something to stop the madness, but her voice box and her feet had shut down. Vee hugged her shoulders helplessly as she tried to fix her mind on the right thing to say.

"Ooh, we in trouble now." Vee mouthed the words to Linda.

"Shit," Linda said, thinking that Alvin was ruining the best trip she had ever had. Before she could say anything, Alvin pushed her inside the passenger side of his car and slammed the door. The Cadillac was stolen, but Alvin called it his own. Linda's dream of flying had turned into a nightmare when she got into Alvin's car. But she admitted that the crushed velvet seats felt so much better than the concrete curb. Her head was spinning.

Now, behind the wheel, Alvin kept his tongue in check but his eyes displayed a bewildered look that scared Linda. Alvin had never been at a loss for words. His piercing stare showed a deep concern like he had lost something precious, especially because Linda was used to seeing the lustful stare Alvin had shown her since they were ten years old.

Linda shook off her high. She pulled down the passenger side mirror to check her makeup hoping that she could refill Alvin's eyes with passion and fire by applying a touch of red lipstick. But his look of sadness had turned to disgust.

"What you staring at?" Alvin said, his big baby browns fixed on Linda like peanut butter stuck on a tablespoon. There wasn't anything sweet about how she felt looking back at him.

What?" she asked softly, hoping to change the mood. "What? What? What you think is the matter?"

Alvin stared Linda down as he drove faster and faster over speed bumps, causing his muffler to drag on the ground. He stared her down, never once looking at the road.

"Slow down. Slow down," Linda pleaded. "Or let me out!"

"Just shut up," Alvin said. "Tell me! What you done had?"

Linda had seen Alvin mad before, especially during those times when he couldn't get what he wanted when he wanted it. He especially got pissed when Linda called him "a momma's boy." He was the baby boy hardly ever denied anything because of his sweet-talking and bullish ways.

His anger today was different, Linda thought. She expected Alvin to slap her face with the back of his hand but he had never raised a hand.

Linda felt a combined tinge of guilt and confusion as he parked the car in a spot behind her building. He threw the gearshift into park with one hand and cupped her chin with his other. He looked into Linda's droopy eyes.

"I knew it," he said nodding to himself. "You using dope. I knew it."

"So," Linda said shamefacedly, acknowledging for the first time Alvin's suspicions. She didn't care that he knew. She had already tried and liked it. If Alvin got pleasure out of using dope, why should she be ashamed?

Why should she be left out? She thought in truth that sometimes Alvin loved dope more than he loved her. Still, his reaction made Linda realize something she hadn't considered before. Doing what Alvin did might hurt their relationship.

Looking in his eyes, Linda saw that Alvin loved her as much as any black man living in Hartford could love the mother of his child. She wanted to turn back the clock, if only for an instant, to feel the heat not from the dope but from the way she felt when Alvin passionately looked her in the eyes before he had caught her 'sperimenting that day on the street.

That look was gone now. What could she do to get it back? Linda didn't know at the time, but the pleasure she found from dope would mean that she would never have all of Alvin's love again.

She would spend the next twenty years trying to get it back.

For now, at least she could pretend that Alvin would get used to the idea that she got high, too, and they could start getting high together. It would make them grow closer, she thought. In the decades to come, they would chase the white powder together, as if getting high was the only thing in their lives that really mattered.

But at this moment, Linda felt like Eve must have felt after she gave Adam a bite of the forbidden apple inside the Garden of Eden. She saw in Alvin's eyes a reflection of her own lost innocence on a level deeper than she ever had before. She also felt sick, dizzy and naked because she yearned to try out the ways of the world and it ended up turning her man against her. Nothing could tell her how to react as Alvin restarted the ignition. She knew that he wanted her out of the car. They wouldn't be going to the back woods in the park to do the nasty, something Alvin always insisted they do when he picked her up.

He didn't act like he wanted her anymore, and Linda wasn't prepared to let go. She held onto the door handle as if staying in the car would reverse what she had done.

"Get yo' ass out of my car," Alvin spat in his voice deep and colorless. Linda felt that he was about to cry because his voice cracked when he said it. She held on. When he grabbed her arm tight, she fought Alvin as hard as she could from the passenger seat. His grip was relentless. From their windows, Linda's neighbors saw Alvin pull Linda out of the driver's side door, pressing hard on the sore places on her arms.

She bit her tongue and tasted her own blood as tears rolled down her cheeks.

"What you fighting me for? You do it! My brother do it! My auntie do it! Junior do it! Uncle do it! Why not me? Why not me?" Linda pleaded as Alvin shut his door, shifted the car in reverse and pressed his foot hard on the accelerator.

"I told you, I'm a man," Alvin yelled out the driver side window. "You can't do what I do!"

Linda refused to let go of the door handle. She held on, trying hard to hold onto her man. She knew that Alvin was mad but figured that he wouldn't drag her down the street, so she clutched both hands around the door handle.

"Hold on tight," she told herself. "Tighter. Tighter."

Before she knew it, Alvin was out of the car, yanking her by her store-brought ponytail like it was a dog's leash and dragging her to the ground. His eyes filled with silent tears and his heart hardened. He pulled Linda by the arm up to her back stoop. He left her there on the ground and marched back to the car. He didn't look back. Once he got behind the wheel, he reversed the car, turned it around and concentrated on the speed bumps. He sped off before Linda, his first love, had gotten up and reached for the handle of the broken screen door.

"Shit!" Linda cursed.

Linda had barely composed herself when she heard her daughter Tanya inside the house, screaming and wrestling loose from the arms of Linda's younger sister.

"That's my mommy," the young child wailed.

There was no time for Linda to grieve her misgivings. Her mama gene kicked in. She got up from the ground and walked inside the apartment.

"Now I got to deal with this shit. What is it?" Linda yelled as her sister held out her daughter for Linda to take into her arms.

"You hungry, baby? Mommy's gonna feed you. Just hush now. Mommy got a headache," Linda said as she placed Tanya on her hip and put a plastic pacifier into the crying toddler's mouth.

Linda prepared her daughter's bottle with government-issued formula and thought about the events of the day. She felt anguish, but a private place inside her mind rested on the promise that her best girl Vee wouldn't part her lips about what they had done. She never factored that Alvin would find out about the 'speriment. Now Alvin had something over her. She wasn't planning on getting hooked. Yet, she knew Alvin would always hold against her the fact that she had shot dope with a needle. That was how Alvin was.

Since the day they first met, Alvin had tried to prove to Linda that he was bigger and better than any other brother on the block. He had always forced his way into her life. If he told Linda's secret to her mother, she would deny it. But she knew he'd be more convincing. After all, Linda thought, Alvin, and only Alvin, was the best, blackest creature that every walked the streets of Hartford.

The thought of losing him hurt her heart.

CHAPTER 4 | ALVIN

LINDA WENT TO AUNTIE ROSIE'S as frequently as she could to escape Mommy and Daddy's madness. At home, all Mommy thought about was getting her "drink on," and that meant more housework for Linda. She and Mommy had an unspoken agreement whenever Linda could tolerate Mommy's madness. If Linda went to the store for Mommy, she would give Linda change for candy, chips, ice cream and grape soda. Linda fed her sweet tooth and Mommy drank until she passed out watching her stories on TV.

Boy, did Linda pay for their arrangement. The house had to be cleaned, the food had to be cooked. Linda cleaned the fat off the chicken parts that Daddy liked and washed all the dirt off the greens that Mommy cooked. It troubled Linda that Mommy would accept the compliments and the pints of liquor from Daddy as thanks. He didn't know for years that he should have been thanking Linda, who did most of the household dirty work. Daddy King saw Linda only as a thumb-sucking child and another mouth to feed.

Staying at Auntie Rosie's during school breaks gave Linda respite. Auntie let Linda sleep late on mornings she would normally be scrubbing, sweeping and standing at the sink washing dishes. Her Auntie liked the way Linda did housework, but she wasn't a slave driver. Her favorite chore was making the Kool-Aid even though she often dropped the five-pound bag of sugar on the floor.

"Over there, I am free," Linda told Vee when she expressed how much she missed her friend during school vacations and on weekends. Vee, a girl with woman-child duties of her own, understood once Linda explained that at Auntie Rosie's she was free to be a budding teenager who could play her records when Auntie Rosie wasn't watching "Gunsmoke" and "Bonanza." She could count on Auntie's telephone because the telephone at her apartment was often disconnected.

"Nobody depends on me over there likes they do at home," Linda said.

It was the summer of 1963, when other young black girls were playing with dolls, realizing a sense of self-discovery or fighting for freedom at civil disobedience demonstrations. But ten-year-old Linda was obsessing about how Tutu's soft lips would feel against her own.

She tossed and turned through the night on the floor pallet she shared with her sister, thinking about her boyfriend from the first month of second grade. Linda made up her mind the following day to act upon her desires. She didn't have to worry about getting caught with a strange boy in the house. Her Auntie had gone to town to shop for Sunday dinner, giving her free time to frolic. Her only problem was, her sister Debbie was also spending the summer with Auntie. She might get ticked if Linda had Tutu over to visit and she didn't have anybody for herself. Her sister would never settle for being made to feel like a third wheel, left alone sitting on the couch in front of the black-and-white TV set.

Linda considered her options while she washed up the breakfast dishes. She called Tutu to tell him that he would need to come over to Auntie's with someone who would show genuine attention to her sister. Tutu promised to deliver within the hour. With no time to waste, Linda primped in the bathroom mirror, applying Vaseline to her lips and baby powder to her eyes, while Debbie looked over her shoulder.

"You want some of this?" she asked Debbie, offering the Q-tip covered with powder.

"Try it," Linda told Debbie, hoping that she would be grateful later for fixing herself up after the surprise stranger appeared at the door with Tutu.

Linda prayed quietly as they dressed in bell bottom blue jeans and tube tops that Tutu would bring over somebody for her sister. But Linda never anticipated that the guy Tutu picked would be Alvin, a fine-ass boy about her age from around the way who had winked at her and tried her patience. Linda heard the knock on the door before Debbie did and opened the screen door to her dismay. There was Alvin standing at the door with Tutu. Linda let them in and pretended that she hadn't met Alvin before.

But Alvin was excitedly bold. He spoiled her secret once he set foot inside Auntie's duplex.

"I want the black one," Alvin blurted out before Tutu could

finish introducing the two sisters.

Linda froze up. She recognized Alvin as one of the boys who started paying attention to her at her family parties in Grandmomma Parkman's basement in "The Square," one of the newer posh housing developments built by the federal government off Main Street. His skin was smooth and took on the appearance of creamy fudge. His processed hair was fine, shiny and wavy, while Tutu was sporting a greasy Afro. Alvin tried pushing up on Linda long before she was interested in boys. He didn't try to hide his attraction to her then, and he certainly wasn't hiding it now.

"I want the black one," Alvin said again so loudly that his declaration confused the couple.

"You know my girl Linda?" Tutu asked.

"Nah, man. Nah," Alvin said. "I'm just playing. She belongs to you?"

"Yeah, man. This here is my girl," Tutu said boldly.

Their exchange gave Linda an opportunity to regain her composure. But she noticed that Alvin's roaming eye was giving her another once over and he made her nervous. Alvin was a determined sort of kid, who acted older than most third-graders. The arrogance and demeanor in his eyes and posture told Linda that he was trouble. He wouldn't give up easily. Their eyes locked again, before Alvin broke the trance between them.

"Ain't ya'll got some Kool-Aid? Can a brotha at least get somethang to drink?" Alvin said, mimicking the older boys who let him hang out with them.

The four of them drank the Kool-Aid in uneasy silence. Linda was fast for her age, but she was afraid of what Alvin might do. She was standoffish and Tutu noticed that something was out of sorts.

Alvin and Tutu didn't stay for long that first day. But the look in Alvin's eyes told Linda that he would be back trying to look under her skirt. She saw triumph in his big brown eyes, something she fought hard to resist.

Linda wasn't prepared to see him or any other boy that following Sunday when Alvin showed up at the door. Her Auntie had left for Sunday school, leaving Linda home alone to answer the door wearing only a thin cotton nightgown.

"Debbie ain't here," Linda said, hoping that Alvin would go away.

"Good," Alvin said. "I came to see you."

"Well, that's too bad," Linda said as she blocked the small opening of the door with her bare feet.

But Alvin was stronger. He pushed open the screen door and made his way inside. "I'm thirsty. Got some more of that Kool-Aid? It sure was good."

He must have seen the purple stains on her nightgown, Linda thought.

"Stay right here," she said as she left the living room and went into the kitchen to pour Alvin a glass. Before she could turn away from the refrigerator, Alvin was standing behind her kissing on her neck.

"Stop. Stop, I said."

Linda pushed Alvin away and marched back into the living room. She opened the front door.

"Out. Get out," Linda said, louder than she wanted.

"Can I at least have the drink?"

He took the glass of Kool-Aid and slurped down the drink. Linda was flattered by how much Alvin loved the sugary concoction that she was famous for.

"Now, get out," she teased.

Alvin handed her the jelly glass without a fight. "Suit yourself," he said, placing his hands up like he had surrendered to her rejection. "I got other girls with better shapes."

The insult stung. Linda was determined as she held open the door. She was ready to slam it in his face once he stepped out onto the porch. But he reached back and brushed his soft brown fingers across her lips.

"You know you want me," he said. "Forget Tutu. Keep playin' hard to get and see where that gets you. Okay, for now."

Linda expected Alvin to turn and leave, but when she released the door Alvin reached around her and pinched her tiny 10-year-old nipples through the opening in the screen. She pulled away as the outer door slammed in his face.

Alvin wasn't discouraged. He walked away with a smirk on his face. Deep, deep inside, both of them knew that Alvin saw Linda's rejection as a challenge. Now, everywhere Linda went she would see Alvin hanging out -- leaning on a tree in the schoolyard, showing up at Grandma P's Saturday afternoon card parties. He would make up any excuse to get next to her and he was getting under her skin.

Once he came into the kitchen where she was. Everyone else at Grandma P's was either in the basement or in the backyard at the cookout.

"So it be you frying that chicken?" Alvin said, standing in the doorway and licking his fingers.

"You again," Linda said. "Yeah, I am the No. 1 chicken fryer round this house. I fix hair, too."

Alvin licked his fingers in a way that told Linda he wanted more than battered fried wings and thighs. He was being nasty.

After Alvin's first visit to Auntie's house, Linda fell out of puppy love with Tutu. She let the other boys in the projects know this by the way she walked, dressed and paid attention to different boys. She flirted in a way that intentionally sent a message she was available, but not to boys like Alvin who took her for granted. If he was jealous, he didn't show it at first. She heard through the grapevine that the ten-year-old tough, who tried to act a lot older when he hung out with the older boys, had told almost everybody in The Square and the surrounding neighborhoods that Linda belonged to him.

"Now, ain't that nothing," Linda thought when the word got back to her that Alvin was claiming her as his girlfriend. Still, she played hard to get and tried not to show she liked the attention that Alvin displayed just about every time he saw her.

One day, when Linda ran outside to catch the ice cream man, there was Alvin, behind the counter.

"We got vanilla, chocolate and strawberry. Let me guess, chocolate?"

"Yeah," Linda said sarcastically. "Chocolate." She smiled.

Alvin continued to show up unannounced. He even came to her house near the projects, expecting that she would loosen up and stop playing hard to get. She got comfortable kissing Alvin but he always tried to take it further. Once, when she snuck outside to see him, she pulled away when he put his hands down her panties. Alvin made it clear to her that one day she would have to "play pussy" with him.

"Oh, you so nasty," Linda told him.

But Alvin fired her up inside, and the feeling confused her. She resisted him and was scared to go to third base, a term she had heard about from the older girls in the school bathroom.

"Why?" Alvin protested. "Why?"

"Cause, Mommy said I can get pregnant if I keep kissing boys. I should be expectin' a baby anytime," Linda said fearfully, rubbing her tummy.

Alvin didn't correct Linda. He didn't know whether what she said was true. He quit for a time until another day, when he caught her at home alone wearing another nightgown. The sight of her tiny breast peeking through the cotton slip was irresistible to Alvin.

He reached out to cup her tiny breast, which she often laughed about with her girlfriends because they were "itty bitty titties." Linda pulled back. She covered her breasts with both hands.

"I'll be right back," Linda said as she raced up the stairs to change her clothes. If Auntie came home and a boy was in the house, she would get a beating. The whipping would be worse if she had on her nightgown. She knew if given the chance Alvin was going to get what he had tried to get so many times before.

Linda made it to the bedroom. She rushed to pull some thick blue jeans out of her laundry bag. She had put on one leg of her bell bottoms before she realized that Alvin was standing behind her, cracking a smile.

He reached behind her and put his hand down there and rubbed it, while he kissed the back of her neck.

"Stop,'" Linda attempted to say, but as she turned around her voice was muffled by his thick hand. Alvin held Linda's balled fists. He knew she would sock him if he let go and Linda broke free.

"Relax," Alvin whispered while she caught her breath.

He kissed her once more, slow and gentle this time, and she kissed him back. She gave Alvin an inch of control and he took over. He pushed Linda down on a pallet of blankets on the floor as she fought the warm feeling creeping inside her underpants. The feeling didn't last. Alvin put his finger down into her private place. Linda wiggled and tried to get away. When she looked down, she realized that it hadn't been his finger at all.

"You done put your thang in me," Linda panicked. "Whoa. Whoa. Stop. Stop."

Linda pushed Alvin off the pallet and onto the bare floor. He flopped back onto the blankets and kept moving on top of her like he did when they slow danced, grinding and moaning as if a love song was blaring from the radio. Linda stiffened her back and tried to squeeze her legs shut. She closed her eyes and pretended that Alvin hadn't stolen her most precious jewels. She felt sore and ashamed and she screamed for help.

Alvin saw the hurt in Linda's eyes and he panicked. He jumped up and back into his pants. Alvin, who had a way of smoothing things over, didn't say anything as he exited the room, ran down the stairs and slammed the front door. He had never done the nasty before, though he heard a lot about it from his older friends, but as he bolted from Linda's apartment he acted like the scared little boy he really was.

Linda thought if she stayed on the pallet and didn't move, she could imagine that Alvin hadn't been there at all. She stayed on the floor for as long as she could, wishing that she could turn back time. Tears rolled down from her almond-shaped brown eyes. She listened carefully to the sounds around her. She heard the other children out back, racing and playing hide and seek. She should have been outside, too, playing hopscotch, jump rope or jacks. But no, she thought, she was "playing pussy" with Alvin, a boy who played the field with other girls. She wondered how many other girls he had tricked into playing the nasty game. Jealousy and fear warred inside her.

After a while, Linda willed herself from the cradle position on the floor and pulled off the sheets and blankets. She didn't want Auntie to come back before she had cleaned up and fixed her a special jug of her Kool-Aid. She inspected the sheets on the way to the bathroom.

"Blood!" Linda gasped.

The bloodstain freaked her out. Once she saw it, she dropped the sheets into the bathtub and ran cold water over them. She grabbed the first toothbrush she saw resting on the face bowl and rubbed the bristles over a bar of Ivory soap. She dipped the brush in a bottle cap of Clorox bleach. She figured if she scrubbed away the spots, she could wash away the pain she felt between her legs and inside her heart. The bleach worked. Once the spot disappeared, Linda ran cold water in the face bowl over a rag and washed her insides as best she could.

Hours passed and Auntie still hadn't come home. Linda sat in the dark considering what to do next. She decided that Alvin would always be her man, even when they got older.

"Him inside me changed me," Linda confided to Vee the next day. Her friend hadn't reached second base with a boy but she nodded her head. She had seen the word "sex" in her science book but she didn't know what it meant until Linda explained what had happened with Alvin. The last thing that Vee's mother wanted was for her daughter to get caught up on the vicious cycle of having a baby before she was ready. She told Vee that only grownups had sex and children who did it would go to a special kind of hell. She said the best thing for her to do if a boy tried to put his hands or anything else on her privates was for her to run like the devil was chasing her. Vee's mother told the story in a very convincing way and it was often the subject of the teenager's nightmares after innocent encounters with frisky boys.

"What you gonna do?" Vee asked Linda once she explained in great detail what had happened.

"I don't know," Linda said.

They sat in silence on Linda's porch until it was time for her to go inside. The streetlights were coming on. The next time Alvin snuck up behind her to cop a feel, Linda didn't run, wiggle or pull back. She didn't fight what Alvin called "playing pussy." She figured if they were going steady, she was supposed to let him have his way.

Mommy was downstairs drinking when Linda let Alvin inside the apartment from the back door. They had regular "lovemaking" sessions inside her bedroom when her brother and three sisters were playing outside. Linda never thought Mommy was alert enough to notice. They were doing it on Linda's bed one afternoon when Linda caught a glimpse of Mommy looking at them from the hallway. She didn't say anything, so Linda kept kissing Alvin. She wanted Mommy to know that she knew that she had lied to her when she said she would get pregnant if she kissed a boy.

Three years passed before Mommy's warning came true. Linda had missed one period and was about to miss another one when Mommy startled her from her sleep.

"Get dressed. We goin' to the clinic," she told Linda.

Linda dressed in haste. She didn't have time to primp. She picked out her shirt and was looking for matching pants when Mommy reappeared at her bedroom door with both hands on her hips. Linda pulled the first pair of pants she saw and put them on. She didn't want to chance getting slapped down. Mommy hardly ever demanded that Linda go anywhere with her, so Linda's stomach jumped with curiosity and anxiety at the same time.

"Get some bus fare out the cookie jar and hurry your fast ass up!" Mommy said.

Linda followed her mother's orders without protest. She checked the jar and noticed that all the crumpled five-, ten- and twenty-dollar bills were gone when they had been there the day before. She wanted to ask where the rest of the money was, but Mommy had a tone of voice that meant business and she would give Linda a hellfire and brimstone beating if she talked back.

Mommy walked out of the front door and down the street for the city bus, walking at a set pace that made it hard for Linda to keep up.

Mommy turned her face to the window and said nothing to Linda during the hour bus ride. Linda wanted to ask why Mommy thought it was necessary for her to see a doctor. But she didn't. The few words Mommy said made Linda suspect that Mommy had counted her Kotex pads. Did she know she had missed her monthly period? She was only 13, and pregnant for the first time.

Other riders rang the bell at their bus stops; the dinging sound broke Linda's concentration. The bumpy ride over potholes on Hartford's raggedy streets jolted something inside of Linda that day. She secretly wanted Mommy to argue with her, so she could exit at the next stop. But Mommy was stone-faced and continued to stare out of the bus window as if she was seeing the city for the first time. Linda stared, too, at the dilapidated apartment buildings, the abandoned cars and heaps of garbage on the streets destroyed in the riots that had swept the country several years after the Rev. Martin Luther King Jr. and Robert F. Kennedy were assassinated. She was happy when the driver drove past a better part of town in an upscale black community near the hospital and to the clinic frequented by poor blacks. The doctors and nurses at the basement clinic looked at Linda and Mommy with disgust and pity as they directed them to a strange-looking bed where Linda underwent her first pelvic examination.

Nothing about this day made Linda feel wanted and cared for. She felt violated and ashamed when the doctor pushed a cold metal instrument inside her private parts. The examination made her feel nastier than any "game of pussy" that she and Alvin had played. She rested her feet in the icy cold metal stirrups and daydreamed of a time when she was still a little girl with her virginity intact. She closed her eyes and dreamed of better days until Mommy shook her into reality and ordered her to remove the backless hospital gown and get into her clothes.

"There is nothing we can do for her here," the nurse whispered to Mommy after the doctor walked out of the room. Linda saw the nurse, who had kindness in her eyes as she slipped Mommy a folded piece of paper.

"Go to this address," the woman said. "They take care of situations like this there."

Mommy nodded and thanked the woman. She looked over at Linda and pointed to the bright red exit sign above the door. As they rode on the bus together Linda thought they were going home, when Mommy rang the bell for another bus stop. She asked the driver for three transfers and reached in her breast pocket for coins to hand the driver. In silence, Mommy and Linda crossed town as the sky signaled dusk before reaching a back alley stretch where hardly anyone spoke in English. Mommy knocked three times as the nurse instructed her. A cherub-faced Spanish woman beckoned them inside.

"Baby?" the woman said.

Mommy nodded.

The woman pointed Mommy and Linda into the direction of

a back room that was dark and smelled stale, except for the candles burning. In the shadow, Linda noticed another hospital bed with metal stirrups, and she feared what would happen next. She drifted off into a haze until Mommy wrestled her awake.

"Get undressed," Mommy demanded.

Linda obeyed.

The procedure was performed by candlelight. Linda saw the needle before the woman stuck her in her buttock. Everything else was a blur. She woke up to the sound of Spanish music in the background as Mommy shook her back to reality.

"Linda! Linda! Let's go," Mommy said. "Get dressed."

Linda looked around the room. For the first time, she noticed pictures of Jesus lining the walls and she prayed that nothing bad would happen to her. The candles were still burning so she could see Mommy when she took the hanky out of her breast pocket and handed the woman a few crumpled bills. Mommy didn't say much on the way home. But when she did speak there was finality in her voice.

"Problem solved," Mommy muttered. "Problem solved."

"Problem?" Linda thought. "All I've ever been in this family is a problem. Now, she done made me kill my baby." But she didn't dare mouth her objections.

Linda thought later that Mommy had taken her to get rid of the baby because a child would interfere with her afternoon bliss. She would have felt better going too far with Alvin if Mommy had cursed her out, made her stay in her room for a few days or let her keep her unborn child. It was over before Linda missed more than one period. They never spoke of the problem again.

Getting rid of a teenager's problem was illegal then. The fact that she had gotten pregnant at thirteen was a secret between her and Mommy and it made Linda nervous that now both Mommy and Alvin had something to use against her. Linda avoided Alvin for weeks after that. When he called, she told her sisters that she couldn't come to the telephone. When he knocked on the door at his regular time during Mommy's stories, she pretended that she wasn't there. Having an abortion was something that she never knew about until that day in the back alley clinic. It was something she never planned to discuss with Alvin or anybody else.

Finally, when Alvin came over and banged violently on the door, she let him in. She feared that Mommy would wake up from her slumber on the couch and find them. She pushed Alvin away when tried to kiss her and she lied that "Miss Mary," the name she called her monthly period, was making an extended visit. She kept him at bay for another few weeks until she couldn't resist kissing him back. She knew where kissing might lead but she was definite about keeping her boyfriend. They messed around under school bleachers, on the basement floor and in Linda's bedroom for three more years. When she got pregnant this time, she was happy that Empire-style dresses were in fashion. The dresses were big enough around her waist and hid the baby growing inside of her naturally petite frame.

Linda thought her secret was safe until the spring flowers sprouted in the dirt outside. She was pressing Mommy's hair in the kitchen one Saturday when Mommy pushed her down to the floor and went into a violent rage.

"Get your pregnant self away from me!" Mommy's voice had

a sharp demeaning tone.

"What?" Linda asked.

"What, my ass!" Mommy's temper was as searing as the hair oil popping on the straightening comb sitting on fire on the gas stove. "Don't what me! I know when Miss Mary comes to visit you and she ain't been to see you lately," Mommy delivered an open hand slap across Linda's face.

Before she could relax, the oil popping inside the teeth of the comb caught fire on the stove. Linda grabbed the wooden handle without thinking, burning her arm and the palm of her hand before dropping it to the floor.

"Shit, Shit, Shit," Linda screamed when the stove top ignited into flames.

That day, Linda stopped worrying about what Mommy would do next. She rubbed chicken grease over the exposed burned skin, an old-home remedy that initially made it feel better. After she wrapped her arm, the injury burned as if her skin was cooking in hot grease. The injury left a permanent burn scar. Linda felt burned twice, by the incident with Mommy and then by Alvin, who had gotten her pregnant for a second time. The sting of the dual injuries made Linda even more stubborn. Linda continued to deny her pregnancy to Mommy with the same vigor she did every time Alvin asked. He couldn't help being curious each time he watched Linda scarf down potato chips dripping in hot sauce and the sour pickles that he bought for her at the corner store on the way to school.

"What's wrong wit you? You pregnant?"

"Nope," Linda said as she shoved down her morning snacks.

"No I ain't!"

"The little birdie don't lie," he said.

"You wanna bet," Linda said.

Her second pregnancy caused a lot of friction between Linda and Alvin. Linda wasn't ready to believe it herself. She expected that at any time Mommy might again wrestle her out of her bed and force her to go back to another backroom clinic to get rid of her child. That day never came. She was forced to face the consequences of being another expectant teenage mother living in a low-rent tenement who worked occasionally as a day laborer, digging potatoes at nearby country farms or counting buttons at the city-run factory. Working, even under the table for less than minimum wage, did not take her mind off her own drama of having a baby without a father. Linda was annoyed by the lack of attention she was getting from Mommy after she was burned, and it hurt her feelings.

She knew that her mother was boiling inside over having to move down the street to The Square after the incident. Linda's only defense was to lash out. She stopped doing her daily chores, exposing Mommy's scam to Daddy King, who expected that his dinner be on the table when he got home. Linda continued to reject Alvin, who was acting like a proud papa with his chest poked out. Her pregnancy was becoming difficult to hide. She felt nauseated all the time and it made her angry.

"It was all his fault," Linda cried as she stuffed soda crackers into her mouth hoping to push back the vomit she felt even on an empty stomach.

Deep down, Linda admitted to herself that "fine ass black

nigger" of hers was going to be a daddy. That fact made her even more determined that because Alvin had planted his seed inside of her, she was going to fix his ass, and good. The signs of her second pregnancy were obvious even to Linda's sisters, who asked why she was always so sick. When her younger sister found her in the bathroom bent over the toilet bowl, Linda continued to lie. "I think it was the food I ate in the school cafeteria," she said, wiping her mouth.

Mommy and Daddy King also had discussed Linda's pregnancy and now they would not leave the subject alone. They called Alvin over to the house one evening when Linda was doing the supper dishes to talk to him about his responsibilities. She wasn't in the room when the conversation began but when she returned to see what they were talking about, Alvin and Daddy King had stepped out onto the porch. Linda panicked. If Daddy King had exposed her secret, Linda would have to face the reality that she was becoming a mother.

Linda went off once Alvin left. She was angry with herself that she hadn't had the courage to tell Alvin first, even though he knew.

"It is none of your business," she told Daddy King. "My baby is my business," Linda stammered.

The conversation was over that night before her parents turned out the lights and ordered everybody to go to bed. But Linda couldn't sleep.

The fact that she was pregnant would never be right with Alvin's mother, who had said once when they brought Linda around that she wasn't the one for Alvin. "Not good enough,"

Linda mouthed to herself when she over head Alvin's mama questioning her baby boy about why he was "chasing tail with that dark chocolate chile."

Linda never mentioned the conversation she had overheard because the thought that someone thought she wasn't good enough made her feel ugly and unworthy of the boy she loved. After Alvin brought her to meet his mother, Linda didn't say much during the ride home. She kept quiet about her feelings. But it hurt inside and she cried throughout the night. Linda's parents were suddenly supportive of the teenage lovers because their middle girl was having a baby. Linda thought about their response, and it bothered her. She figured it out during one of her sleepless nights. The proud grandparents were not as happy about having a grandbaby as they were about getting another check from The Welfare.

State law prohibited sixteen-year-old girls from taking care of babies by themselves. Her parents saw the money coming, her money, Linda thought. She kept her suspicions about their motives to herself. Linda was pressing Mommy's hair the following Saturday when the subject of her pregnancy came up again.

"So, what you gonna do?" Mommy probed.

"I don't know," Linda responded.

"Well, you better think on it. Time waits for no one."

As she blew onto the piping hot comb, Linda accepted her predicament. She accepted that she was "expectin", as they called it. She knew that getting knocked up had hurt Mommy, who hated the spotlight being shined upon her household by nosy neighbors, who always had something disparaging to say about her middle daughter. Linda knew she had to make amends in her family as the pressure around them mounted. As she parted Mommy's bangs into an s-curl on her forehead, the final touch to her hairdo, Linda promised her mother that her first child would be her only illegitimate baby.

"I ain't goin' be one of them girls having lots of babies by lots of different mens. We gettin' married if we make another one, okay?" Linda said.

"If you say so," Mommy said as she got up and left the room.

CHAPTER 5 | CRAVINGS

ONCE THINGS SETTLED DOWN with Mommy and Daddy King, Linda struggled to concentrate on her next move. The baby growing inside of her was taking over. The pickles, pomegranates and ham sandwiches that she craved warred inside her bloated belly and forced Linda to confront the toilet bowl. She didn't have morning sickness but twenty-four-hour sickness, and nothing she did stopped the violent eruptions throughout the night. The wrenching and loud sounds of Linda's vomiting in the family's only bathroom were enough to wrestle even Mommy from her bed to check on her.

"You alright in there?"

"Yeah," Linda lied as she wiped the vomit from around her lips.

Linda laid down on the cracked floor tiles after Mommy walked out of the bathroom shaking her head in disappointment. The cold floor gave her comfort as she drifted in and out of sleep. She was exhausted by morning but she forced herself to get up and to dress for school.

The school for tenth-grade pregnant girls was different from regular high schools. The teachers there anticipated that the girls would miss classes and didn't send out the truant officer to investigate when they were absent. Linda picked through her clothes in her section of the closet she shared with her sisters. She selected one of the most attractive Empire style dresses that concealed her pregnancy. The smell of bacon frying in the kitchen made her sick to her stomach, and she repeatedly made trips to the bathroom to splash cold water on her face. She pushed away the feeling long enough to put on her dress. She went downstairs and took a seat on the plastic-covered sofa while she forced her mind to concentrate on anything other than being pregnant.

Alvin blew the horn outside. Even though Linda knew that Daddy King had talked to him about the baby behind her back, and a blind man could see that she was pregnant, she still refused to acknowledge it to Alvin for her own selfish reasons.

Alvin was smiling when Linda took a seat beside him in the Cadillac he'd bought from yet another greedy used car dealer. Linda was always amazed that her boyfriend could buy a car even though he was only 16 years old and didn't have a driver's license. The Cadillac, like all of his other cars, was big and flashy and unregistered with the state. He sat behind the wheel and pretended to be a super pimp, dressed dapper in a matching suit, hat and wing-tipped shoes. He always parked down the street from where his family lived in a three-bedroom apartment in the nicer part of the projects, so he wouldn't need to explain where the car had come from and who sold it to him without his parents' permission.

His momma would force him to take it back if she knew. She would say Alvin was too young to be buying cars. She still treated him like a baby boy, but once Alvin stepped outside, he assumed the demeanor of a grown man and he fooled a lot of people.

He was proud of his new tomato red ride with spit-shined white-wall tires and the polished dashboard. He knew that if he was caught driving without a license, the boys in the black-and-whites would immediately force him to spread eagle across the hood of a cruiser before taking away the keys.

Alvin was an adolescent speed demon. Linda nicknamed him "Leadfoot" the first time she rode with him. This particular morning, Alvin was in one of his moods, though he still play-ing the role of Linda's private driver. He had quit school and fooled a lot of people who were confused about his age. Nobody asked him why he was hanging out when most boys his age were reading the classics, bagging groceries, fighting in Vietnam, or marching in the Civil Rights Movement.

"You like?" Alvin said, stomping his foot on the gas pedal and making the engine purr.

"Yeah. It's nice," Linda said as she painted on a wry smile with a tube of dime-store lipstick. She applied the makeup as her decoy. She purposely tried to distract Alvin so he wouldn't no-tice that she had hiccups. Each time she tried to swallow back, the vomit forced its way up from inside her swollen belly into her throat. Linda's facial expression gave her away as she settled in the front seat. She held onto the door handle and prayed that she could keep it together until she reached the girl's bathroom at school. She fished out some soda crackers from inside her pocketbook and shoved them into her mouth. She was praying that her stomach would calm down as the wheels of Alvin's car struck water-filled potholes.

"So, is you pregnant?" Alvin asked as he turned off the radio.

He pushed harder on the accelerator when Linda didn't answer. He was agitated.

"That was my song," Linda protested.

"Answer my question! After all these months, I had to find out about my baby from Daddy King," Alvin said.

He drove faster, hoping to scare a confession out of Linda.

"Nope," Linda whispered.

Linda and Alvin, who were born months apart, both had stubborn genes. She refused to give Alvin the satisfaction of the truth. She was afraid and upset that her naturally petite body was steadily growing out of shape.

"I know you is. I knows it," Alvin said as he drove faster around the corners.

The ride felt as if they were traveling on two wheels. Linda hated it when Alvin drove this way. She poked out her lips and folded her arms around her unborn baby.

"You is!"

"I ain't!"

"You is!"

"I ain't!"

"You is, goddamnit! Why can't you say it? It will be all right. Just say it," said Alvin, who was growing even more heated that

Linda was denying his seed in front of his face.

"I don't know," Linda answered.

Alvin wondered to himself after his conversation with Daddy King whether it was a boy, another chocolate brown wonder taking Hartford by storm. But the pleasure he had about becoming a father was confusing now as he argued with Linda. They battled like that until Alvin reached Linda's school just five minutes later at the rate he was speeding. When they arrived, the car skidded to a stop and he parked on the sidewalk instead of the available parking spaces, drawing attention to them when Linda wanted only to rest her mind and her stomach before going inside to face the teachers. It seemed to Linda that the baby was becoming more important than she was. Nobody asked her how she was doing anymore.

"How's the baby?" the teachers asked. The concern they paid to her unborn baby made Linda feel invisible and unimportant at a time she felt she needed their attention the most.

"What about me?" Linda wondered aloud.

She felt a strange jealousy toward her unborn baby that she couldn't explain. Linda could not deny her pregnancy once her abdomen grew to about the size of a small watermelon. She needed new clothes. The dresses that hid the baby were getting tight around her butt and waist.

Once Linda admitted that she was pregnant, Alvin teased Linda about becoming a "fatty." When he was normally absorbed in his cars, drugs and other girls, Alvin became generous and protective on the weekends. He didn't complain when Linda asked him to take her shopping at Woolworth's, J.C. Penney or G. Fox or the Sage department stores. But they continued to argue for months about whether they really had a baby on the way.

Her on-again and off-again denials were grounded in other worries. She was expecting at a time when respectable young girls in the 1960s who didn't get married were shunned for not keeping their legs closed. Older women in Linda's neighborhood openly gossiped about girls like Linda, who they called "fast" when they had let aggressive boys like Alvin go too far. Linda knew this. She knew that being a pregnant teenager from the projects struggling to get out of the tenth grade gave her a permanent reputation. Her first child would be labeled a bastard or illegitimate, which was a dirty phrase in those days. Nobody in the Negro community wanted that shame.

Linda thought if she didn't talk about her baby on the way, she could hold off the gossip. What was done was done. She fought her worries about the social pressures but, in reality, she was concerned most that the baby was taking charge of every aspect of her young life. When she should have been going to school, dancing at parties or getting high in secret, Linda was responding to her cravings. And when she wasn't hungry, she was sleepy, angry or sick. She refused to eat the bagged bologna and cheese and soggy tuna sandwiches from the school's cafeteria. She snuck out of the back of the building and waited for Alvin to race her to the Copaco Jewish deli on North Main Street to satisfy her appetite.

"Give me one of them pomegranates," Linda told the man behind the counter. It seemed like every day, all day, she asked for a piece of the rare fruit when the season permitted. Her cravings were so controlling that she hoarded the strange fruit in her oversized pocketbook. She liked sucking on the seeds better than soda crackers. It got so bad that even Grandma P teased Linda about turning into the ruby red fruit with the sweet seeds.

"They taste like candy," Linda said sheepishly, hoping that Grandma P would not say anything about her baby. When Linda wasn't eating the ruby red fruit, she begged Alvin to bring her ham grinders and potato chips that she drenched in hot sauce. She gorged on grilled government cheese sandwiches and spoonfuls of peanut butter. Pomegranates, ham grinders and grilled cheese were all she wanted when she wasn't biting down on a giant dill pickle she fished out of the jar sitting on the deli's counter. Food made Linda forget about how much she hated being pregnant, though she paid for the smorgasbord of her unusual cravings late at night. Linda gobbled down her food from the deli but struggled to keep it down later in the day.

Alvin was oblivious to this. He drove so fast that her stomach felt like she was being taken on marathon roller-coaster rides.

"Pull over," Linda screamed during one of these rides.

"What?" Alvin said as he turned down Bobby Womack on the radio.

"Pull over!"

Alvin slammed on the brakes with both feet and pulled the car to the curb, and Linda jumped from the passenger door. She vomited right on the street. Once she got back into the car, Alvin had slicked the paper on a freshly rolled joint with his tongue.

"Here, smoke this," Alvin said.

"What?"

"Smoke this."

The weed settled Linda's stomach and she felt better, not embarrassed about what Alvin must have felt about her vomiting on the street. The sick feeling returned once she went back to school, and she vomited in a paper sack that she kept in her desk drawer. Her sickness would not let up and it got so bad that the following morning, when Alvin appeared at her doorstep, Linda told him she had quit school.

"Quit? Quit? You quit?" Alvin said. "I got my ass up in this weather and you quit! You could have called a brotha. I know that pay phone still work outside. I woke up to take you over there and now you quit."

"Yeah. This baby is doing flips and I can't stand going no more. The chairs is hard. My butt be hurtin' all the time," she said. "I'm sick, Alvin."

Linda knew that he was high but she didn't press the point. It had become a daily routine: he was smoking reefer and popping dope into his veins when he wasn't doing pints of beer. She didn't ask Alvin about why he was high all the time because he was still trying to take care of her and their baby on the way.

"I guess he celebratin'," Linda once told her friend Vee.

Alvin's binges didn't matter so much to Linda when he showed up grinning like a proud daddy carrying arms full of clothes for her. She was superstitious about getting baby clothes before the child was born. She had heard that it was bad luck. What if the baby was stillborn? The clothes would be a sad reminder of the hell she had gone through from the time the child was conceived.

It had been a rough week for Linda.

"Um, um, um," Mommy said before slamming the bathroom door shut without asking her about her condition. "Told you, when you play with fire, you get burnt."

It was cliché that Linda literally understood.

Linda was unable to respond at that moment. But the incident inside the bathroom kept her wondering about what Mommy would do about her problem. Later, when Linda went downstairs to find something to eat, Mommy was sitting at the kitchen table with her hands folded across her chest.

She was pouting and Linda expected that Mommy was going to curse her out. She didn't feel like hearing it, so she thought of something that was pleasing.

"You ready for me to do your hair?"

"My hair? You got nerve prancing around her like everythang all right. So, you grown now? I see you. Let's see how far you can make it with that bastard you is carrying. It ain't going to be easy, you know."

"But Mommy ..." Linda protested.

Mommy placed her index finger up to her lips, indicating that she didn't want to hear Linda's side of the story.

Linda finished putting her chips into a bowl and carried it into the front room where she had planned to watch TV. But she couldn't focus.

Mommy's words had grabbed something deep inside of her and her belly flip-flopped. The baby was responding to Linda's emotional state and it was kicking so hard that she doubled over. Linda stumbled back into the kitchen as Mommy was finishing up a cigarette. She didn't say any more, and Linda didn't feel like arguing. She went upstairs into her bedroom, a private space at this time of day, where she could release the hurt she felt inside. Disappointing Mommy again hurt so much that Linda retired to her side of the twin bed and rested her cheek on the concrete wall.

CHAPTER 6 | DADDY

LINDA'S BLUE MOOD CONSUMED HER. She slept so much that weeks turned into months. Snowflakes had covered the ground outside before she knew it. She dreamed about being a female urban street fighter with a destiny to prove Mommy wrong. She could be a good mother, Linda thought, despite what everyone was saying behind her back. She held on to her courage until Mommy wrestled her awake.

"Get yo ass up! Get dressed. We got some place to go!"

"Where?"

"We got a long overdue trip to the meat market. Just do what I say!" Mommy said as she left the room.

"The meat market?" Linda repeated to herself. Why was she going some place to buy expensive meats when the booster, who sold cheaper stolen meats, was a regular at their apartment? Questions popped into her head but as she searched for something appropriate to wear, there was no time to ponder anything but the kick-ass look on Mommy's face.

Linda dressed hastily into the only dress that fit her bulging waistline. She moved so fast that she nearly stumbled down the stairs when she reached for her coat.

"Damn," Linda cursed after she buttoned her worn overcoat, which barely fit. She tried to be more careful when she bent down to pull up her rubber boot. There was no time for her to sew on the rest of her loose buttons. Mommy was holding open the front door when she looked over the banister.

"All dressed," Linda yelled. "I'm coming."

Mommy didn't look back. Linda stepped out onto the porch and prayed silently that the snow that had fallen overnight wasn't as deep as it looked. She walked gingerly, hoping that the ice wasn't solid. She struggled to keep up with Mommy as the wind smacked her in the face. Linda wanted to turn back, but kept up her sprint behind Mommy as they headed toward the bus stop.

"Pick it up! Let's get to stepping!" Mommy said.

Despite Mommy's brisk pace, a shiver overtook Linda's bloated body before the "C" bus approached. Linda knew better than to complain about the chill and the unexpected trip. She followed Mommy's lead, not saying too much, remembering her sour mood. She noticed that the bus was coming and it calmed her nerves. Linda slid her coins into the fare slot and took her seat next to Mommy without saying a word.

She wanted to ask why it was so important for them to go to the meat market on such a chilly and snowy day. But fear kept her in check. She stayed quiet like that until Mommy rang the bell signaling the driver to stop, and walked to the back exit of the bus, expecting Linda to follow her lead like a dutiful daughter. They crossed Main Street and stood for what seemed like an eternity until the "D" arrived to take them to North Main Street.

Trips like this with Mommy were rare. Linda could not remember going anywhere alone with Mommy, except to the clinic or during their annual journey to the social worker at The Welfare. The unusual trip made Linda feel special and adventurous in a strange sort of way, especially because of the mystery surrounding their going to the meat market when nobody in the household had hit the number at the beauty shop.

The walk was long and scary. As their feet crushed the ice, the danger of it all brought Linda back into reality. It was days like today that Linda wished she had been nicer to Alvin. He might have given them a ride if Mommy let him. Mommy's mood was as chilly as the wind blowing outdoors. Linda was so close to Mommy once they made it into the market that her shoes pinched the back of Mommy heels. She stamped the snow and ice off her boots and onto the store floor covered with wood shavings.

"Damn," Linda cursed so loud that the folks at the nearby counters eyed the pregnant teenager with looks of contempt.

"What you say?" Mommy asked.

"Nothin.' I mean, I'm sorry. Sorry," Linda said, looking down at her feet.

Mommy zigzagged through the oversized market as if she shopped there every day, picking up day-old bread and bruised tomatoes. She paused at the sign decorated with picnic-table red and white checks. The owners had the city's freshest cuts of beef, lamb chops and pork on display inside the clear glass counter.

The tall chocolate-complexioned man behind the counter in the blood-spattered apron caught Mommy off guard. She looked at him as if he was the man that got away. Linda saw something in her eyes that made her think that Mommy wasn't always the drunk who slumbered on the couch in front of the rolling TV screen. Linda recognized the man, too, but she couldn't place his face.

"A sight for sore eyes," he said.

"Yea, it's been a long time, Harry."

"How you?" Harry asked.

"Just fine. Just fine," Mommy lied.

She didn't mention how much she missed him or the good times they had when they were kids. She didn't say how her only real comforts these days came from a bottle of vodka and a pillow on the couch. Her wry smile was a decoy, hiding the fact that Mommy's life was a mess.

"What can I do for you ladies?" the man said.

His generous nature, welcoming smile and hearty laugh made him different from most men Linda had met. She instantly wanted to like him, especially because Mommy was giggling in a way she had never seen before. Linda also saw a distant sadness in Mommy's eyes, the same blue and mellow gaze she had when "Down Home Blues" played on the eight-track.

"This here is my daughter, Linda," Mommy said, breaking the trance between them. "She sixteen. As you can see, she is expectin'. " Mommy was nervous, and she bit her nails. Linda could tell that she needed a drink.

The man behind the counter didn't notice. "How you been, Edith?"

"Oh, I'm alright. Pretty fair, thank you."

"I know you said you didn't come for nothing. But let me fix up something for you, on me," said the man, who hadn't taken his eyes off Mommy.

The man nodded at Linda in a genteel way, as he might greet a young lady on the street. He smack-kissed her on the back of her hand. Linda giggled and Mommy blushed. She hadn't remembered meeting a man with such grace. While she recovered from his flattery, the meat man packed dozens of pork chops, beef tips and chicken parts and wrapped them into thick white paper. He smiled at Mommy in a way that made Linda wonder about the hidden message between Mommy and the dark chocolate skinned man. Now wasn't the time to ask.

"Linda, Linda," Mommy said, gaining her attention.

"This here is Mr. Harry," she said as he handed over two paper bags brimming with meat. The satchels were heavier than any other food bags that Linda could remember. Linda figured that Mommy had some sort of deal with this man. They had something going on, but she couldn't recall where she had seen him before. Something was up, Linda thought.

Mommy generally preferred the cheaper day-old meats, or meats stolen by the booster, who hawked them for bags of dope. Mommy wasn't the sort to splurge on anything other than 80 proof generic brands of vodka.

"See ya 'round," Mr. Harry said. "Can I see her sometime?" he asked Mommy.

"Sure," she said. "You know I told you before. Anytime."

"Nice to see you, young lady," he told Linda.

Linda wanted to say something equally as kind and proper but all she could manage was a smile. She held on to that feeling as best she could.

The walk back to the bus stop was even more troublesome for Linda after Mommy handed her both bags of meats to carry once they had reached the outside door. Rain had slicked the sheets of ice covering the sidewalks, complicating their trek to the bus stop.

"Oh, Jesus. Oh, Jesus," Linda prayed aloud as she tried to balance each step without falling or spilling the meat packs onto the ground. Fortunately, she avoided falling.

Mommy hugged the bags of meat on the bus ride home. They seemed to give Mommy warm comfort and lift a burden from her light- caramel-colored face. She was almost smiling, an expression that was foreign to Linda, who was itching to ask about Mommy's relationship with the meat man but dared not to.

"That there was your real Daddy," Mommy said.

"My real Daddy?" Linda whispered.

"Yeah. Your real Daddy," Mommy confirmed. "We dated when I was a girl before he went away to the Army. He liked me just fine, took me on picnics and everything. He had dreams for me that I wasn't ready for. He came out to the farm, brought me clothes and begged me to finish high school in Simsbury, the only school near where we lived. He thought I should do more with my life. But I was just a farm gal back then. I allowed him to have his way with me. That's how I had you. I'm telling you now because you goin' need your real Daddy when the times get rough. You got a baby on the way," Mommy said.

"My real Daddy," Linda repeated.

For once Linda felt like she belonged. The truth about her real father made sense of the horror that Linda had called her life up to now. As she looked out of the window, frosted with ice, Linda thought of the chores she had been forced to do since she was a little girl. She always felt that Daddy King and Mommy treated her like a Cinderella stepchild who was forced to cook, to clean and, most importantly, be Mommy's responsible house-maid when she should have been outside with her other siblings jumping rope, playing hopscotch or reading fairy tales.

Daddy King had always expected more of Linda than his two younger daughters and his only son. Linda always felt deep inside that he acted differently toward her; now, she knew why. Mommy had dipped into the well of adultery when she was young. Daddy King had come along and was unwittingly duped into putting his name on Linda's birth certificate.

Linda's own reflection in the mirror told her for years that she was different, someone else's child. She was darker than Mommy, Daddy King and all the other children in the family. Linda now resented the man she had called Daddy King since she was able to speak.

"My real Daddy," Linda whispered.

Those three words gave her comfort. She wanted to scream it so everyone on the bus would know that she was somebody's child, somebody who could have loved her if he had been al-lowed to spend time with his only daughter.

"Hush now," Mommy warned. "This is our secret, ya hear. Keep your damn mouth shut!"

Later that night, as she drifted off to sleep, Linda repeated those words quietly to herself, as if she were counting sheep.

"My real daddy is Harry Hartie. His name is Harry. Harry. Not, Daddy King. Harry. Daddy Harry." Linda dreamed of the dark chocolate wonder, who had given her family food. His gesture was something she cherished.

Her real daddy was an honorable man who hadn't learned of her birth while away in Germany serving in the Army. He was somebody who immediately showed that he cared for her mother by the way he packaged the meat in expensive white paper. Now, Linda was expecting his grandbaby. She wondered if he would treat her with the same charm he had when they had met. No other man had before. She couldn't quit thinking about the kind man with a generous heart. Her feelings put new pep in her step, even though she still had to fix Daddy King's dinner and clean his toilet bowl.

Her morning sickness seemed to ease as she said the words to herself, "I got me a real daddy. Okay!"

Mommy told her later, in another quiet moment while they were watching the afternoon stories, that her real Daddy had been her true love. He lived on the other side of town in a middle-class neighborhood, where single-family homes outnumbered the red-brick tenements dotting the impoverished neighborhood where Linda's family lived. Daddy Harry was different from any other man Linda had met on Main and Garden streets where she lived, and where her Grandmother P stayed on Windsor Street. He was a man who obviously loved hard. She knew this each time she went back to the meat counter for packages he had stored away for her mother. Other times when she ran into him on the street, he gave her a handful of silver dollars to save for the baby and more "pocket chain' " to spend on herself.

Linda daydreamed about how her life might be different to-day if Daddy Harry had known Mommy was carrying his baby. Mommy said fear kept her from revealing her pregnancy. If she had said something, Mommy often wondered if he would have married her and pulled her away from Daddy King and from ghetto life.

Linda learned later from Daddy Harry that he had met her mother in 1944 when he came to Granby to pick tobacco with other Hartford youth. He was about 14 or 15 years old, and she was a year younger. "They used to send the truck into Hartford and pick us up and we'd go out to pick tobacco," Harry said later.

Mommy's family lived on the farm with six or seven impoverished families who had migrated to Connecticut from the South. They were there year-round, working the land. At some point Harry talked Edith into graduating from Simsbury High School. He rewarded her by paying for her yearbook and clothes for her graduation. Graduation was a big deal in the Parkman family.

On the Fourth of July in 1952, Harry, Edith, his cousin and her boyfriend went swimming at Battison Park in Farmington. He tried picking up Edith to throw her into the water and she drew away. It was the first time he suspected that their relation-ship would crumble before his eyes.

"What is wrong with you? You pregnant?" Harry asked, even

though they had never had intercourse.

"Nah, I'm not pregnant," Edith lied.

But Harry wondered. He had purchased hundreds of dollars worth of fireworks that he promised to take back to the kids on the farm. "That's why the kids loved me," he said.

When they returned to the farm, Harry tried touching his girlfriend again. "I went to grab her, like I usually do. And she pulled away from me. 'You been doing this all day. You pregnant,' " Harry said.

He took her home and asked to speak to her mother in private.

"Mrs. Parkman. I think Edith is pregnant," Harry said.

"What ya'll goin' do?"

"It's not mine. I don't touch her like that," he said.

That night after he set off the fireworks, Harry offered to give the family five dollars, so Edith could go to the doctor. He left that night knowing that his suspicions would be confirmed the following day.

After Mommy had her first son, she told Harry that a guy named Buster had pushed up against her when they were fooling around and it went too far.

The Parkmans, Sims and Shannons would share family ties. Edith married King Shannon after Harry Hartie went into the Army in 1951. Edith wrote Harry often, but he rejected her advances when he went away to Germany with the 82nd Airborne. She had gotten married and was having her second baby. Edith did everything she could to keep Harry's interest. She sent a photograph of herself in one of her letters. A friend saw it and asked if Edith had any friends that she could hook him up with.

She offered to set Harry's friend up with her aunt, who was staying in Springfield, Mass., less than an hour from Hartford. His friend was eager to meet Edith's aunt when he and Harry returned home to Connecticut for Christmas.

"Why don't you take a ride with me?" his friend asked.

Though Harry was tired, he took the road trip with his friend to meet Edith's aunt. Edith was there, too, and he tried ignoring her. It was clear that he was exhausted from the trip, and a little drunk, when Edith's aunt suggested that Harry take a nap. "Go in there and lay down," she said.

"I got sleepy because I was tired. I went in the room and lay down,"

Harry said years later. "When I woke up, I was almost naked. That was the first time I had ever touched that girl sexually like that. I had done little things but I was not having intercourse with Edith."

After the holiday, Harry left Hartford and went to Texas. He was working in the motor pool when he got another letter from Edith.

"You smart son of a bitch. You thought you was smart. I finally got you. You thought you was so smart and you was going to get away from me. I am pregnant and it is your child," Edith's letter said.

Harry responded with anger. "You are a silly, stupid person. How do you think you could get back at me? You are carrying the baby," he responded.

Edith wrote Harry again in January. She said she had been

to the doctor and the baby was due in September.

"Stop writing me," he wrote.

When the baby was born, there was no way Harry could deny that Linda was his child. She looked a lot like him. Edith had kept a good relationship with his mother and she told her that King was "mean to her."

She said she turned to liquor and to anyone who would spend some time with her. "She wouldn't even drink with me. She became a total alcoholic," Harry said.

That was the only mother that Linda knew. Mommy's blues had sealed her fate. She covered up her heartbreak with pints of liquor she brought with spare change from her monthly food stamps. Mommy realized that she had settled for the lesser man who worked at on-again, off-again construction jobs while she sewed buttons on war garments. Staying with Daddy King in the two-bedroom apartment in Bellevue Square they moved into after the stove fire never raised them out of the economic bottom.

In the beginning of their marriage, Mommy felt the only way to hide her secret love was to seduce Daddy King, even though the fire in their love life had long since been reduced to a flicker. She could never let that soft-spoken country man who turned into a raging madman when he was liquored up find out she was carrying another man's baby. He would beat her up and send her packing. She turned to alcohol to ease her feelings of regret.

Daddy King didn't know he had been deceived until after Linda was born around lunchtime on September 25, 1952, at Hartford Hospital. He was giddy about seeing his daughter, peering through the looking glass in the colored section of Hartford

Hospital for the child his wife named Linda Carole Shannon. When the nurse held her up, he felt dizzy from the alcohol. He rubbed his eyes to get a closer look and he was surprised that his new daughter child had deep chocolate skin, the color of a candy bar.

Mommy's secret was revealed. He knew immediately that Linda wasn't his child. She didn't look like any of their other children, who bore his signature caramel complexion, pug nose and oval eyes. Mommy denied it later when he asked her during an argument how long she had cheated on him.

"Case closed," she said.

CHAPTER 7 | MOMMY

ALVIN WAS THE PERFECT EXPECTANT FATHER and provider. He had practiced his boosting skills at the Sage Allen and G. Fox department stores downtown. He boosted clothes and even baby formula when he couldn't come up with another hustle. He stole other items, too, which he returned for cash so that he could buy a rocking horse and other toys he thought his baby needed. It was clear by what he brought to Linda's door, before the baby was born, that he was expecting a boy. No female child would play with toy guns, marbles, G.I. Joes and footballs.

He thought he had fooled the police and store security officers who followed him around the department stores. They were so eager to arrest Alvin that they posted his picture inside the cash register drawers. The store detectives warned the cashiers that Alvin was a crafty thief with a cunning smile and quick hands. He could conceal just about everything inside his big coat or a shopping bag, they said.

Alvin thought he had beaten the system. He detested the government for not providing enough money from The Welfare to buy his child's clothes. The system had put him into a position where he had no other choice but to steal. He made a joke out of his many capers. He laughed under his breath each time he left a store with a bulge under his overcoat.

"Hey, hey, hey. Goodbye." Alvin was humming the popular tune to himself when the black-and-white police cruisers turned on the sirens and stopped his car. The trunk was stocked with diapers, clothes, pins and pajamas for the baby. He had no choice but to surrender when he noticed both patrolmen had their hands on their guns.

"Y'all got me fair and square," Alvin told them. "Fair and square."

Alvin's daddy days were over just about the time Linda's Mommy passed suddenly. Her liver exploded one day as she was taking her morning siesta on the couch. Nobody was pre-pared for her death, especially Linda, who was bonding with her young child born in December 1968. Daddy King wasn't pre-pared to live without a woman he had grown to love, even if the love was dysfunctional. He hadn't been much of a parent and he didn't want to learn now.

On the morning of Mommy's funeral, Linda came down-stairs expecting Daddy King to be passed out on the couch. She had laid out his black suit the night before, and ironed the stub-born wrinkles from his one white shirt. Daddy King was in the kitchen on the telephone. He had his back to the door and didn't hear her enter.

"She grown now," he said. "Time for her to get a place of her own to stay for her and that baby. Nah, he goin' to his Momma P's house to live. I'll keep my two girls."

Linda couldn't figure out who Daddy King was speaking to

but she understood that her time under his roof was coming to an end. She ducked out of the kitchen and into the basement to sniff the last pinch of heroin she had hidden in her housecoat pocket. She started using the strong narcotic once Tanya was born and a friend brought a surprise package to her in the hospital. The high calmed her nerves, helping her escape from the shock of her Mommy's death.

When her high wore off, her thoughts went back to the day ahead. She joined her sisters in the car that took them to the funeral and to the gravesite. Most of the day was hazy. But she remembered standing by the open ground when the gravediggers lowered the pine box containing Mommy's body. Tears streamed down her high cheekbones until her cry turned into a moan. She tried jumping into the grave, but the pallbearers carried her back to the car kicking and screaming.

The reality of losing two parents in one day was confusing. Linda approached Grandma P, who was dishing up plates of food for the mourners who came by her house to pay their respects.

"Just for a little while," Linda begged.

"Now, you know that this ain't the proper place to bring this up," the elderly woman said, looking at Linda over her eyeglasses.

"This 'posed to be the day of yo' Momma's home-going. But I will tell you this, I ain't got no room for you and yo' baby," she said in a hushed tone. "I'd take ya brother cause he can sleep on the couch and keep them bad ass boys from round my door at night."

Linda knew better than to turn her back on Grandma P,

but she sure felt like it. She willed the tears welling up in her eyes not to fall. She thought about Mommy lying in her prettiest dress buried in her casket. Tears dropped from her eyes and she wanted to holler.

But Linda had never raised her voice to Grandma P and she wasn't going to do it now. She knew the old woman would slap her face right there in front of everybody. She already felt humiliated and unwanted, so she simply nodded her head.

"Gal, you listening to me?"

"Yes, Mama," she said.

"What about that boy's family. Can't they help you some?"

"Yes, Mama," Linda said.

She was too embarrassed to tell her grandmother what Alvin's mother had said about her years before. She knew she would never sleep under that woman's roof.

That night Linda returned to Daddy King's house. She was restless as she thought how Mommy was buried in a poor man's grave. Mommy went to church so irregularly that the family had to hire a preacher from the tiny storefront near the projects to conduct the eulogy. The preacher knew so little about Mommy that he kept mispronouncing her mother's name as Edina. It agitated Linda.

"Edith Parkman," Linda wanted to yell, but she knew better than to make a scene. "Edith was her first name. Edith, bitch."

As the gravediggers shoveled the dirt over Mommy's body encased in a pine box, Linda thought of how Mommy would have wanted a memorial stone that, at the very least, would have said that she tried to be a mother, a grandmother and a wife, that she had loved and been loved, no matter how flawed her life had been.

Though she tried, Mommy had barely bonded with her granddaughter Tanya, who was already walking and talking. She emerged from her alcoholic haze when she gave the baby regular baths.

Linda felt desperate when many of the mourners left for their cars. She cried on the shoulder of Alvin's sister, a reliable friend, who took Vee's place when she moved to Georgia. Alvin was now the property of the state, so he couldn't help plead her case with his family. It was clear that Daddy King wanted her out of the family's house in the Square. He came home one week after Mommy was buried and left empty boxes outside the front door. Linda heard through the grapevine that Daddy King had told Mommy's family that Linda's presence reminded him of Mommy's infidelity. He didn't want her bastard child living with him anymore. Grandma P took in her brother, but not Linda.

"Ain't blood supposed to be thicker than water?" Linda asked Alvin's sister.

"I don't know," she answered.

Suddenly Linda's fairy tale of a home for her new family came to an alarming halt. She was a single mother without the means of taking care of her own child without full assistance from The Welfare. Linda ignored the boxes and avoided Daddy King until she could come up with a plan. At night, after she put Tanya to sleep, Linda's mind kept trying to figure a way out of her desperate circumstances.

CHAPTER 8 | HOME

THE SUN BROKE THROUGH THE CLOUDS that Indian summer morning, revealing God's overnight handiwork. He had used his paint brush to dot New England's tree-lined streets with touches of fire red, burnt orange, yellow and muddy brown. The last of the warm weather seemed to call her outside as Linda dressed Tanya, placed her in a used stroller, and rolled her out of The Square.

The streets were empty except for the day workers at the city bus stops on their way to suburban mansions, and professional men who circled the streets near the highway off ramps looking for their favorite drug dealers. Linda watched as the corporate executives in their Brooks Brothers suits picked up bags of dope to lift their spirits later in the day after attending boardroom meetings inside the nation's most prominent insurance companies. She wheeled Tanya away, hustling through the side streets until she happened upon a brick apartment building that she liked.

A placard in the picture window read "For Rent" in big block letters. Linda knew this would be her first place. Daddy King was getting on her last nerves. Now, when the postman delivered the monthly welfare check bearing her dead mother's name, he forced Linda to sign the government stipend over to him. Just before Mommy died, she stayed sober enough to subtract the cost of Tanya's milk and Pampers. Linda ended up with the change. Though she never protested, she grew resentful every time she noticed Mommy's cookie jar spilling over with tens and twenties balled up in a tissue. Linda felt she had earned every dime every time the bleach and ammonia she used to scrub the floors made her eyes tear up and her nose run.

She gritted her teeth when she got on her hands and knees the way Mommy taught her. She had been exploited as a cheap laborer at the expense of her dignity since she was a little girl. Nothing changed after Mommy died, Linda thought. She felt imprisoned by Daddy King's rules. Linda was upset when she rolled Tanya up to the red-brick apartment building with the vacancy notice in the window. The sign gave her hope and she immediately visualized the possibilities of gaining her freedom. She would need to buy curtains for the large picture window, a bed, sheets, towels and a sofa.

Getting all those things would be tricky, she thought. She'd need to concoct an elaborate story of mental and physical abuse at the hands of Daddy King if she wanted help from her social worker.

She jotted down the number on the sign and called her worker's number from a pay phone. The receptionist said her worker was busy with other clients and wouldn't be available for at least a week.

Linda was satisfied with the news. She spent the next seven

days plotting her strategy. She woke up early on the morning of the appointment and dressed the part of a desperate single mother about to get put out on the streets. She dressed Tanya in her best outfit, but the dress Linda wore was patched and tattered. Her shoes were worn slanted heels bought for five dollars at the thrift store. They hurt her feet so badly that she was walking with a limp by the time she followed the social worker down the long concrete corridor.

"You all right?" her worker asked as she took her seat behind her chair in an office cubicle.

"Yeah," Linda said sheepishly.

"What can I do for you today?"

"He say we can't stay there no more," Linda said. "Me and my baby goin' be on the street if I don't get help."

"He who?" the worker asked.

"Daddy King. He ain't my real daddy but I stay with him. He be real mean to me since Mommy passed. He say if I don't scrub the floors, wash his clothes and cook his dinner, we goin' be out. He be fightin' me and everythang. We need some place of our own."

Linda's story seemed credible to the social worker, who knew her family's history. She felt sorry for the teenager. If she were in danger, the worker knew she had to help. If she ignored the girl's plea, and Linda got hurt by the man who had been labeled in the file as an abusive father, she might end up on the street herself.

The worker handed Linda a tissue to wipe away the fresh tears on her cheeks. "I'll see what I can do to help,"

"I really need your help. Tanya need it too," Linda said as she grabbed her toddler's arm away from the candy jar sitting on the woman's desk. "Stop it," Linda said, louder than she wanted. "Don't touch."

"It's okay," the worker interrupted. "She can have a piece." The worker made a mental note of how Linda had grabbed the child.

Linda's tone and threatening manner didn't escape her. This child is afraid, the worker thought.

"Ask first," Linda said.

"Canna I? Canna I have candy?" Tanya stammered.

"Sure baby, take a piece. That's a good girl."

"What you say?" Linda yelled.

"Thank you," the child answered.

The experienced worker kept her cool. She expected Linda to take the wrapper off the treat, or at least show the child how to unwrap the candy. They both watched as Tanya chewed through the paper. She liked the taste of the hard grape candy and sucked it like a thumb. She licked the paper with her fingers, now sticky and wet, before wiping them on the front of her dress.

"Now, look what you done," Linda said.

The worker noticed Linda's lack of instruction and attentiveness. She had criticized the child but failed to wipe her hands before she put her bony arms through the thin cotton coat, which was inappropriate for this time of year.

Government work made her jaded. She had grown tired of young women with babies ruining their futures. She learned long ago that young women like Linda were too hardened to listen to her advice. She stayed behind her metal desk taking mental notes that this single mother was like a long line of others. Linda needed to be taught to become a nurturing parent if she was going to make it on her own out in the world. If she didn't get help, this toddler would be in front of another social worker once she reached puberty, carrying her own bastard child.

"Give me a call tomorrow," the worker said. She made another mental note that Linda had not asked for the things she needed to put a home together. "Think about what you'll need to make this work," she said. "Make a list."

The city welfare department offered services for indigent mothers, such as vouchers for furniture, clothes and money for meals until their food stamps application was processed. The worker didn't volunteer any of this to Linda. She wanted this young mother, desperate for her freedom, to stew over her decision. If she thought she was capable of running a home, city welfare would become her new Momma and Daddy. The assistance would come with a demoralizing cost that she didn't feel like explaining to Linda, a young woman raised on food stamps and welfare checks. The government could be as mean and agitating as the man she called Daddy King.

Linda bit her lip in anger and held her tongue when she realized the worker wasn't going to tell her the rules up front. Her great escape, she thought, was more important that getting into a fight with her worker. She kept her cards close and also held her tongue.

"Time somebody else picked up my heavy load," Linda muttered to herself later in the day as she scrubbed the floors and baseboards. The thought of being emancipated made her smile. She felt for a minute that she was related to the fabled Cinderella character, even though she knew deep down that Alvin would never become her prince. She had grown more than sick of the daily routine as a servant who never reaped any rewards.

"Room and board," Daddy King said one day after overhearing her complaints. "You ain't got no choice but to earn your keep, ya hear. If you don't like it, get to steppin'."

Linda kept her peace and saved her pennies. She had a baby who was sweet as a chocolate bar when she wasn't crying for attention. Accepting the responsibility of caring for Tanya came with sacrifice. She did her chores without complaint and worked part time on the sly digging up potatoes at a nearby farm. The work was hard, but the money was good, an investment for her own 'partment, as she liked to call it.

Linda never liked dirt. It seemed to her from the time she could walk and comprehend that her job was to erase dirt and grime from the walls and floor from her parents' apartment. Now she was digging potatoes, the dirtiest job she had ever had. She did her woman-child duties as diligently as an indentured servant and kept her job at the farm secret from her social worker at The Welfare.

Her great escape would be ruined if she found out Linda was working. Daddy King had accused her of stealing money when he found it balled up in the bottom of the cookie jar. She didn't have the heart to tell him that Mommy had socked away the money before she died, and she shrugged off his accusations.

The fifty cents a burlap bag she earned had doubled since

a boy sweet on Linda filled her burlap sack with more potatoes than she could carry. Linda's shoulders ached at the end of each day and the pain in her belly she felt every time she left the farm perplexed her. She didn't know why the farm work made her sick to her stomach. That sick feeling would take years for her to sort out.

Linda shrugged off her discomfort most days on the farm, perspiring under the blazing sun, and daydreamed about her future. Her hard work paid off three months later when she signed the papers for her place on Mansfield Street, a tree-lined street of multi-family Victorians and three-story apartment buildings. Hard-working people had scrapped their way out of the projects by working at the gun and airplane factories to live here, she thought.

The nice brick building she chose had two bedrooms, a bathroom and a kitchenette. There was a laundry in the basement shared by five other families.

"A perfect six," the landlord had called it when he gave her the keys after she showed him the papers from her social worker. The papers proved that she could pay the rent with government assistance.

"A perfect six?" she asked.

"Yes, young lady, that's what we call these buildings because there are six apartments in each building. You ain't going to have no wild parties, are you?"

"No sir, I want this 'partment' for me and my baby. Her daddy is away," Linda said.

"Away, huh? Well, we don't want no trouble."

"Yes, sir," Linda answered politely. "No trouble."

Linda wrote Alvin at the state penitentiary about her plans during a moment between her work at home and on the farm. He had matriculated from the city jail after being sentenced to the state prison at Cheshire. A lengthy bus ride took Linda to see him behind the plastic glass and her heart ached every time she visited. She missed Alvin's touch and his voice, because the prison telephone crackled with static. They were reduced to small talk when Alvin had broken the rules and were denied conjugal visits inside the prison trailer park.

The five-story prison housed hundreds of men in tiny cubicles behind metal gates. The food was terrible and the place smelled of the urine inmates regularly threw from bottles at the guards as they walked by.

Alvin worked in the kitchen as a potato peeler. He often traded snacks from the commissary for bags of sugar, which he mixed with potatoes to make the prison wine everybody called hooch. The money he made paid for cigarettes, toiletries and an occasional candy bar. If Alvin stayed out of trouble, he would be coming home to their 'partment in less than a year, Linda thought as she sealed her letter. Once she told Alvin, her man, telling anyone else wouldn't be a problem.

Though she didn't immediately hear back from him, Linda felt confident once she had unveiled her plans. She knew that Alvin would be happy about sleeping in his own bed, paid by the government.

The following night, Linda fixed a dinner for Daddy King. When he had eaten and sat back with a beer in his hand, she made her announcement.

"I'm moving," she said.

"Say what?" Daddy King said, belching up his meal.

"I doubt that," Linda's brother interrupted.

"Oh, yeah, I'm out of here," Linda said confidently.

Her sisters laughed in unison as Linda cleared the table, still acting like a dutiful daughter.

"I'm goin' to have the last laugh," Linda quietly smirked.

"Say what?" Daddy King slurred, a tinge of meanness in his voice.

"Nothin," Linda said, hopefully quieting the storm that she felt brewing at the table. "I ain't said nothin."

"I didn't think so," Daddy King said with a finality in his voice that made Linda sure he would slap her down if she expressed herself any more assertively.

Linda knew better than to talk back. She broke the tension in the room thick with uneasiness as she turned away the tub of water in the sink filled with scalding hot water for the dishes. Her mind drifted back to the quiet place where she daydreamed. Her apartment was a place where she could drink her own liquor and take a hit of dope on the weekends without having to slip into the cold dark basement. She had discussed her great escape with Vee over the telephone and with her trusted Auntie. They were familiar with Linda's desire to be free of Daddy King's demands. Vee and Auntie were especially encouraging when they found out that she could furnish the place without spending any of her savings or asking them for loans they knew she could never repay.

The Welfare would become "big Daddy," the ultimate provider who would fork over the money for Linda and Tanya's rent, milk, Pampers and groceries. Linda would use the change she made on the side for her weekend escapades at the dope house. She was exhilarated. Nothing Daddy King could say would bring her down. She was on her way to accomplishing mission impossible.

Linda bundled up Tanya once she got a break, put her in the stroller and took her to her Auntie, a trusted babysitter. From there, she took the bus to churches and charities she had visited with Mommy when she was looking for handouts, to gather hand-me-down clothes and toys for Christmas. Linda was overwhelmed once she made it to the Salvation Army store. It had everything for the kitchen, bathrooms and bedrooms, all the things she needed. But her excitement cooled when the elderly clerk tapped her on the shoulder.

"You need some help?" the woman asked, wearing a wary smile.

"Huh?" Linda noticed that it was the same woman who had assisted Mommy years before.

"Hi, miss. I need a bed, some sheets, some towels, some pots, some dishes..."

"Hold on, little lady," the clerk said. "Let's get one thing at a time. Is this your first place?"

"Yeah," Linda said, grinning with embarrassment. "I'm getting' me a 'partment."

Linda's excitement was infectious and the woman smiled. "Congratulations," she said.

They picked out the linens, moved to the dishes and pots until they ended up in the furniture section. Linda picked out a firm bed and a sturdy dresser. She was exhausted on the bus ride home, but her mind was in high gear.

Linda didn't have a dependable ride home once Alvin got locked up. She had no choice but to carry two heavy bags filled with linens on three city buses. The clerk from the Salvation Army promised to deliver the furniture and dishes to her apartment once she was ready. The Welfare worker had given her a voucher and she didn't have to pay for the items in cash. The generosity of the government was a sign to Linda that she had made the right decision. Linda could make a home for her family before Alvin got home.

That night, she got on her knees, something she didn't normally do. She knew deep down that Alvin was a felon and an addict, two things that always made him unreliable, and she prayed that her man would work with her once he was released. She asked God to remove the nagging doubt, that once he got home, he'd go back to drinking and drugging and would never straighten up.

Would Alvin abandon her in every department except the bedroom?

Would she be left a single mother fending for herself with the man who had an unrepentant passion for easy money?

She pushed those feeling into the backside of her mind.

"Please God," she said, knowing that it would take divine intervention for Alvin to become a man and a father.

CHAPTER 9 | OLD HABITS

LINDA DID THE FUNKY CHICKEN, the popular dance of the day, when she walked into the spacious living room of her new place. She kept up her groove as she unpacked her record player and stack of 45s, her most prized possessions. The music helped her keep pace as she cleaned and scrubbed every nook of the apartment. Mopping, dusting and scrubbing away the scum left by the previous tenants didn't bother her. This was her place, a new home for Tanya and, once he came home, for Alvin.

Little Tanya stayed over at her Auntie's until Linda got everything in her apartment situated. "Do your thang girl," she said when Linda asked her about babysitting her daughter.

"I'm crazy bout my sweetie," Auntie said as she pinched Tanya on the cheek. Linda gave Tanya a tight hug and quickly bundled up. The cold air outside kissed her cheeks as she carried brown packages filled with linens, clothes and new curtains.

Throughout the day, Linda felt that her woman-child days of servitude were coming to an end. She felt responsible for the first time.

She tried to prove that fact to herself, if even in tiny superficial ways. The curtains she picked out matched the paint in the two bedrooms, one for the baby's room and one for the room she planned to share with Alvin. The inside of the older style building was classic. It had brick walls in some places, making it easy for her to play her hi-fi as loudly as she wanted. She was in love with Marvin Gaye and Donnie Hathaway's music. Both were dreamboats who sang about love and the times of the day. She sang along to their songs until she memorized the words so she wouldn't be embarrassed when she and her friends got together to serenade one another. Linda was loud and sang off tone inside her apartment. She wrapped her arms around her shoulders imagining the time when Alvin would be home.

After a day of cleaning and unpacking, Linda checked the mail. She was excited when she saw the postmark for Cheshire prison, and even happier when she found out that Alvin was coming home in ninety days. Linda realized after reading the first few lines that it wasn't a happy letter. She felt the sadness in Alvin's words. His tears had made the ink run on the plain white paper.

Alvin's mother had passed away while he was behind bars. The state Department of Correction made him go to the funeral wearing a bright yellow jumpsuit, handcuffs and leg irons around his ankles. The warden rejected his requests to change into his street clothes. He imagined that he should have been wearing his Super Fly apple jack-style hat cocked to the side as he strutted into the church. Instead he could hardly walk in his trademark stride. The prison knocked him down to a humiliating level.

The warden made Alvin feel the sting of prison. His angry

words in the letter made Linda upset and sad. She wanted to hug him tight and wipe away the tears she knew had formed in his big brown eyes as he wrote to her. She gripped the letter in the palm of her hands and kissed the envelope, wishing it was Alvin's sweet chocolate lips. Linda folded the letter and tucked it inside her pocketbook. She stared into space for the rest of the night and ached for Alvin's touch.

For the next three months Linda focused on making her apartment perfect. She was meticulous about making sure everything stayed clean and in place. She coordinated the curtains and rugs in the bathroom so they matched with the baby blue tile. The ruby-colored rugs matched the kitchen tiles. She was proud. But only Alvin's approval would seal her conviction that she was becoming a real woman, not a girl pretending to be grown.

She exercised her freedom at night when she went out partying at the American Legion, the Cleveland Café, Benny Long and Jerry Mack's on the Avenue and a couple of hole-in-the-wall joints on Park Street. When the cheap liquor didn't do the trick, Linda slipped into the bathrooms and got off inside the stalls.

Finally the day of his homecoming arrived. Linda woke up early and put on her best clothes before dressing Tanya in the clothes she normally wore to church. They caught the bus and transferred three times before they arrived at the bus station to meet Alvin. They were looking good, smelling good, and the Vaseline on their faces made them shine like new money, Linda thought, as she held Tanya's hand. Alvin hadn't expected them, but the look on his face showed Linda that everything was right with them.

"Damn, baby, you looking good," Alvin flirted.

"You don't look so bad yourself," Linda flirted back.

"Don't he look good?" Linda asked Tanya, who hid behind her mother's dress.

Linda pulled her closer and rolled her eyes. "Stop now," she warned. "This here is your daddy."

"Daddy?" Tanya said.

The toddler wasn't sure what the word meant but she had seen pictures of this man on the nightstand by Linda's bed. Her mother kissed and massaged that same face each night before they went to bed. Tanya began jumping in place on the sidewalk.

"I got to use it," she cried. "I got to use it. Mommy, please. I gotta go now."

Linda grabbed Tanya by the hand, upset that the toddler was soiling her good clothes. "I told your ass to go before. Now, you done peed in front of Alvin."

Tanya walked as fast as she could, but she could help looking back at that man that Linda called her Daddy.

"I sorry," Tanya cried. "Sorry."

Alvin seemed amused. He lit a cigarette and shook his head at the spectacle.

"Ain't no way that chile going to sit her wet behind on my lap. Pissy," Linda overhead Alvin say. "Pissy Girl."

"Now, you done ruined everything," Linda scolded. "You better stop that jumping around fore you get it."

Linda was enraged when she and Tanya entered the public toilet. It was filthy. Linda didn't like changing Tanya in a bathroom like this. She ran the water until it turned clear, and washed up her baby's bottom with a coarse paper towel. By the time they made it back to the city bus stop, Alvin's sister was driving up to the curb. Linda was relieved.

"A sight for sore eyes," she heard his sister say as she rolled down the window. "Get in this car and give me a hug. I brought you some new clothes, something I think you'd like."

The shirt she had brought for Alvin had a fashionably wide collar. The bell-bottomed pants would hug his hips and he smiled as he felt the thick denim.

Now, Alvin could relax, Linda thought. He wouldn't be caught dead strolling down the street wearing his old clothes because it would show that he had been down on his luck. "You brought the shoes?" Alvin said, without saying thank you.

"Nah, they didn't have your size. Guess you gotta to wear them prison boots you got on your feet," his sister joked.

"Fat chance," Alvin said.

He wasn't the kind of guy who wore last year's fashions. He would get him some Huggy Bear platforms, even if he had to steal them off of somebody's feet.

"You sure is a hard man to please, Alvin," his sister teased.

Before she could finish her big sister speech, Alvin tore open the brown paper bag filled with his new clothes. He disrobed right in the car and threw the prison-issued jeans he hated out of the car window.

"You ain't changed a bit. Always, a baby boy," his sister said.

They rode in silence. Alvin looked outside the car window

for signs of change in the city's landscape since he went to prison two years ago. When Dr. King died, folks in the North End of Hartford took to the streets rioting and burning city buildings for miles until they reached the state's Capitol. Alvin was disappointed that he had missed the action that unfolded in the early 1970s. Still, Hartford was home, he thought, as they passed his favorite chicken shack near the bar, his old stomping ground near Linda's new place.

As they approached Linda's new apartment, Alvin instinctively cased the building like a professional burglar. He counted four fire escapes outside of her neighbors' apartments, thinking that he could easily check them out once he got a spare moment. Prison had a way of teaching young criminals to hone their skills. He was popular in the joint not only because he worked in the kitchen, but because he stole bread and sugar from the kitchen to make hooch. There wasn't enough alcohol in it to get them drunk but it took the edge off and softened even the hardened criminals, who openly bragged about committing even more daring crimes once they returned to the streets.

Linda had never been to prison and didn't have a clue about what Alvin was thinking. She imagined the look on Alvin's face was his gratitude that she had gotten a place for them with the Welfare's help. She wasn't a thief. She silently loathed anyone who would steal from her or put what she had in jeopardy. The thought that Alvin would be casing her building had never entered her mind.

"Nice place," Alvin said when Linda took him inside the building.

The gigantic foyer had mahogany banisters and stained glass windows and significant historical character.

"You think so?"

"Real nice. Better than I thought. You done good, girl," he said as he looked at the mailboxes, noting that all six apartments were occupied.

"Way better than The Vil and the Square," Alvin said, referring to two nearby government-assisted housing projects.

Linda was so excited that she nearly tripped when she sprinted up to the third floor landing. She had already fried some chicken wings and thighs for Alvin. He grabbed the choice pieces before he took off his jacket.

"Got something to drink?" he said as he chewed a mouthful of food.

Linda poured Alvin a glass of Boone's Farm wine that she had chilled in the refrigerator. The look on his face was priceless.

"Slow your roll, before you choke," she said.

Alvin put his index finger to his mouth as he continued to chew the chicken down to the bone. Linda didn't argue.

"Don't you want some bread?"

Alvin nodded and resumed eating. He sopped the grease that collected on his plate with the Wonder Bread slices Linda gave him. He ate nonstop until he cleaned his plate and wiped grease from the corners of his mouth with the back of his hand.

"You eating like somebody goin' steal your food," Linda joked. "Slow your roll."

Alvin grunted, displaying his satisfaction with his first real meal after two years. He belched before resting back in the chair. Tanya crawled on the floor until she reached Linda's ankles and climbed up on her leg.

"Mommy," Tanya wined. "I hungry."

Linda picked up the toddler and hoisted her on her hip. She placed Tanya in her high chair and snapped it shut. Alvin had claimed all the chicken legs, so she slapped jelly on an end piece of bread and handed it to Tanya. She was just as satisfied as Alvin had been gorging on the chicken. Tanya was licking her fingers when Linda pulled away her tray.

"Time for your bath," Linda said. Tanya groaned.

Linda bathed the child and put her into bed at record speed. When Tanya resisted, Linda pulled off her belt and wrapped it around her hand. "You want some of this?"

"No," Tanya said.

"Well, I bet' not hear a word out of you," Linda said before closing the door, leaving it open just a crack, because she knew Tanya was afraid of the dark. "Get your ass out of bed if you want to and I'll give you a beating of your life."

Tanya let out half a whimper. Linda had making love on her mind and she refused to allow Tanya to ruin her mood. She rushed back into her bedroom, the belt still wrapped around her hand.

"You try it tonight and I'll give you something to cry about."

Tanya wiped her little eyes and took one look at Alvin, who walked into the room from the shadows of the doorway. He seemed amused by her antics. Alvin kissed Tanya once on her cheek and tapped her on the behind.

"Do what ya Mommy say or you'll have to deal with me," he told Tanya in a voice that suddenly made her obey. She nestled her head in a pillow and went to sleep.

Once Tanya was down for the night, Linda and Alvin went back into the living room and got busy on the couch. He had daydreamed for two years about being romantic with Linda. He thought about slow kisses and long protracted lovemaking, but all he wanted now was to get off. He forgot about foreplay as he undid his pants and climbed inside of Linda. His gyrations were so hard and forceful that Linda pulled away.

"Hey, wait. Slow down baby," Linda said. "This might be better if we got into the bed."

"Probably so," Alvin said. "But not yet."

He climbed back on top of Linda until he moaned with satisfaction.

"Damn baby. Damn baby," Alvin said.

The thrill was gone before Linda knew it. She never got the chance to put on her see-through nightgown and her sexy slippers. Alvin fell asleep on top of Linda with both eyes closed. She wanted to move, but she stayed there for hours concentrating on his heartbeat. Alvin is at peace, she thought.

For the first time, Linda saw a different man, somebody she could really fall in love with. He was different from the other Alvin. He wasn't chasing dope or plotting how to get some. He was asleep, apparently feeling a sense of safety in her place. Linda imagined that once he woke up he would be a changed and rehabilitated man. She pushed him over, got up and went back to bed with that on her mind.

She woke up early and cooked him a manly breakfast. Alvin woke up to the smell of bacon and eggs frying in a pan. As he ate, slower this time, he looked around and dreamed up what he would steal to get his first fix.

The demons of a dope fix had chased his dreams since he went away to prison. He couldn't get high and buy something for Linda with the measly thirty bucks a month he received from working on the prison gang and as a mess hall cook. After paying off his cigarette debt from his hooch profits, Alvin left prison with only three hundred dollars.

The toaster looked new, he thought, as did the TV and record player. Stealing from Linda was something that Alvin could do easily, but first he wanted to see what her neighbors had.

It was time to make some real dough, he thought.

He spent the next few days sleeping, eating and savoring his freedom. On the morning of his caper, he crept out of bed, slipped out of the front door and surveyed the building occupied by people who had boarded buses to work before daybreak. He picked the locks of each and took every appliance he could carry to pawn. Linda neighbors came home from their blue-collar factory jobs and immediately suspected that the new man in the building, who carried the swagger of a thief, was stealing the toasters, TV sets, and radios they had purchased with their hard earned money. The elderly woman upstairs had spotted him on the fire escape through her transparent curtains as she ironed her husband's cotton boxers. She dropped a dime on Linda with the folks down at The Welfare.

She told the operator that Linda had a regular gentleman caller who had moved into her building months after she rented the place.

"He the one," the woman pronounced to the operator before hanging up without giving her name, address or telephone number.

Linda had no clue about where Alvin was getting money for the dope they were using. The rag doll he brought for Tanya and the brightly colored polyester mini dress he had given Linda was much more than he could afford. Linda knew this, but she was happy that he was once again trying to be Big Poppa, a man who took care of his family, or at least provided them with the things they liked.

Linda was changing Tanya's diaper one morning when the social worker knocked unexpectedly on her door. The woman, who had been friendly before, was bossy that day. She barged her way past the living room and looked in Linda's closets without her permission.

"What you looking for?" Linda asked as calmly as she could.

"Men's clothing," the social worker answered sternly.

"Don't no man live here."

The social worker eyed Linda over her bifocals, turned her back, and just kept looking. She swept her eyes over the room before pulling out the contents of Linda's drawers and dropping them onto the bedroom floor. Linda sat down on her bed with a look of disgust. She prayed silently that the woman wouldn't ask her to move her skinny legs so she could look under the bed.

Alvin kept his stuff there, in a cardboard box as tidy as a service-man. She thought if she sat there the woman would concentrate on the drawers and closets.

Her trick worked. The social worker came up empty. She left in defeat.

"Stupid bitch," Linda cursed once she slammed the door.

She smiled to herself. She had fooled the worker who had hoped to catch Linda in the act of cheating The Welfare.

In those days single mothers like Linda who received gov-ernment checks kept their men on the down low so their checks and food stamps would keep arriving in their mailboxes.

Linda's confidence was deflated days later when two police officers banged on her door. The sound of the billy clubs strik-ing the outside wooden door frightened Linda out of her sleep. The sound was so loud that Linda thought they would bust out the windowpanes of her beautiful French doors if she didn't un-hook the latch.

"Police! Open the door!"

Linda got up quickly and hid the candle, bottle tops and needles that Alvin had used the night before to shoot his dope, before tipping out for the night. He hadn't come home, some-thing Linda was suddenly thankful for.

"Are you Linda Shannon?"

"Yes."

"Does Alvin Jordan live here?"

Oh, not that again, Linda thought.

"Nope," she lied.

"Well, we need to search your apartment."

"For what?" Linda asked sarcastically.

"We are investigating burglaries in this building," one of the officers said.

Over the course of a month, her neighbors were robbed of toasters, TVs and record players, the officer explained. Linda was dumbfounded that the police thought that Alvin had been stealing that stuff.

"I ain't stole nothing. Just me and my baby girl live here," Linda protested.

The officers marched passed her as if they had a right to be there. They opened up her closets, cabinets and doors. Their determination to find something made Linda nervous. She was certain they'd find Alvin's things under the bed.

"I done told ya'll I ain't no thief," Linda said. She followed the officers from room to room before planting herself on her bed. When their search turned up nothing, the officers spoke to one another as if Linda wasn't in the room.

"If we come back here, your black ass is going to jail," one of the officers warned.

Linda looked at the officers with disgust. It took all of her strength not to tell them what she thought about them barging into her apartment so early in the morning. She hadn't even brushed her teeth, and she didn't like how they looked at her body through her thin silky nightgown. She had hated cops since she watched them on TV turning fire hoses and siccing dogs on black men, women and children during the riots and demonstrations across the country. Things in Hartford weren't any better, Linda thought. They showed their contempt for her on their faces.

Police here had earned a reputation for shooting down flee-ing suspects just because they had the power to do so. The be-havior of officers like these had prompted the riots more than the brutal slayings of Martin Luther King and Malcolm X.

"You must have the wrong 'partment," Linda had said.

"Yeah, right," one of the officers said.

Linda felt depressed. She closed the door and slipped back under her sheets. Fortunately, Tanya was at one of Linda's rela-tives and wasn't home to see the commotion. Linda slept be-cause she wanted to get up with a different frame of mind. Did Alvin really steal those things? If he did, would she have the courage to confront him?

This was her first 'partment," Linda murmured. Alvin ain't got no right.

Linda slept through her afternoon stories. She went to sleep feeling afraid, but convinced herself that the worst of it was over. But her luck had run out. Two weeks later her landlord, an el-derly white man with beady eyes, knocked on her door with the same force of a billy club striking the door.

"You got to go," he said.

"Why?" Linda asked.

"You know why."

The landlord said he had grounds to put her out. He said he didn't need to give her any notice. The following day he placed a white sheet of paper under her front door.

"Notice to quit," the paper said.

Linda didn't know what that meant, so she called Auntie for

advice.

"It mean he putting you out,' she said. "Pack your things. You ain't got no choice but to leave 'fo they put all your nice stuff on the street."

"Damn," Linda cursed when she hung up the telephone.

She sat on the sofa and waited for Alvin to show back up. She was so happy to see him that she fixed him dinner. She waited until he rubbed his belly before she confronted him about the allegations lodged against him by the social worker, the police and the landlord in his absence. She hoped that he would deny what they had said, but Alvin shrugged his shoulders.

"Fuck what they say," he said. "You goin' believe them over me."

Linda crushed the eviction papers into his chest. She was ready for a fight because she knew that Alvin had ruined everything.

"Why?" she screamed. "Why?"

Alvin never admitted to burglarizing her neighbors. He acted as if their losses were no big deal. Not his problem, he said.

For him, it wasn't. He had permanent digs at his sister's on the other side of town. He had two places to lay his head.

"My sister say we can stay with her," he said.

"Your sister?"

"Yep. Let's get the hell out of here. I can't stand those nosy motherfuckers, always peeking at me through they curtains. Always up in my business."

Linda was dumbfounded. Did Alvin set her up for this? she thought.

Alvin sold all of the electronics in Linda's apartment and anything else that wasn't nailed down. He didn't seem to care that it was Linda's place and she had put a lot of effort into establishing a home for their family.

"We don't need all that shit anyway," Alvin said. "Let's go. Get the rest of your shit. We don't live here no more."

Linda suppressed her anger, held back her tears and followed the orders of the man she loved. He had left her with very few choices.

"Hurry up," he yelled. "Get your shit and let's go."

Linda grabbed as many of her clothes and Tanya's clothes as she could stuff into brown paper bags. She felt defeated and wanted to fight and to argue about losing her 'partment, which she had spent time and money decorating.

"Come on, or I'm leaving your ass," Alvin said, with anger in his voice.

Linda took the few knick-knacks she could from the antique cabinet built into the wall and stuffed them into bags. She had no choice but to leave the pretty curtains, sheets and matching towels she had spent so much time putting into place before Alvin came to live with her. His commands snapped her out of her depression but she felt a need to escape in the only way she knew how.

"You got some dope?"

"Now ain't this a bitch. You mad at me for bringing in the money so you can get your high on, but you hate how I get it. I'm goin' give you a little taste and that's it. Ain't this a bitch. Now, you want my shit. Just sniff the shit so we can get the fuck out of here," Alvin said as he threw a tiny plastic bag her way.

Alvin didn't worry that Linda would rat him out because he knew that she honored the rules of the street. But he knew that staying around her place would be too risky. Linda tucked the baggie into her pants pocket and followed Alvin to the door. She stepped into the entranceway and looked back at the apartment she had made into a home if only for a short time. Though she fought it, the tears that had welled up in her eyes fell down her cheeks as she looked around. The pillows that matched the drapes were still on the sofa as were the coasters on the coffee table. The room looked perfect, Linda thought as she looked at the second-hand china dishes still on the shelves in the pantry.

"Damn," Linda cursed. "I can't have shit." She thought about whether she wanted to pack up or to move out leaving everything in its place.

"Boxes," Linda said aloud. "I need boxes."

Alvin blew the horn outside while she contemplated her options. "Shit," Linda cursed.

She slammed the front door hard enough to rattle the panes in the French doors. The sound could be heard around the building. Linda looked back as she exited the door and noticed that her neighbors were watching from behind their drapes. She marched toward the front door with a determined look on her face before focusing on her flat metal mailbox. She turned the key as one nosy neighbor after the next eyed her down as she passed the mailboxes in the lobby. She held her breath as she prayed silently that that none of her neighbors would blame her for the burglaries. She had nothing to do personally with the stolen toasters, TV sets and record players, but her stomach pinched with guilt. She held her head down as some of the hard-working men and women eyeballed her. She felt guilty. Shame enveloped her body as she fished though the stack of mail.

"Bingo," Linda mouthed the word to herself as she noticed that The Welfare had sent her monthly check and a hundred dollars worth of food stamps. "Bingo."

She wouldn't be dead broke and hungry while she figured out how to regroup. The financial windfall made Linda over-joyed right up to the time she stepped outside of the building. Her mood changed drastically as she replayed the recent events in her mind.

She was in an overall funky mood once she approached Al-vin sitting in his new ride. Her money and things had paid for this, Linda thought.

"Damn!" she said once she slammed the car door.

CHAPTER 10 | MAKING A DEAL

LINDA LOOKED BACK. She focused her eyes once more at the picture window in the three-story building she had called her 'partment.' She saw the sheer white drapes and thought of how delicately she had hung the photographs of John F. Kennedy and Martin Luther King on the dining room wall. She wanted to weep. She had placed those dollar store pictures inside her apartment with special care. She left them there as reminders that she had created a showplace for her family.

But that was all over. She was homeless, she thought, as she folded the big brown envelope bearing the government seal that she had received from The Welfare and slipped it down her shirt and into her bra for safekeeping. The last thing Linda wanted was for Alvin to know that she had received her check. If he knew, he would charm her into giving him seed money to buy more dope. She shut her mind down from the pain she felt as she got inside Alvin's car and slammed the door.

"Damn girl," Alvin complained. He watched as she settled her tiny frame into the sofa velvet cushions of his new deuce, a big flashy car made by Oldsmobile.

"This here is my new ride," he said.

"Yeah, right," Linda responded sarcastically.

Her expression and body language mirrored the blues she felt so Alvin didn't press the moment. He sped off and blew his car horn, showing his contempt for her neighbors.

"I need boxes," Linda mumbled as tears rolled down her cheeks. "Can we stop and get some boxes?"

Just saying the word boxes tore her up inside and caused tears to fall from the corners of her almond-shaped eyes. She wiped her cheeks quickly. Alvin hadn't responded but he turned up the car radio. He didn't want to listen to the drama unfolding. His answer to the problem was easy, and he handed Linda another tiny bag of dope. Linda took the bag. The white powder might ease the trauma she felt when her landlord refused to listen when she tried to explain that she didn't know anything about the burglaries.

Now as she sat in the crushed velvet seat, Linda didn't have the heart to press Alvin into confessing that he was the thief. Dismantling the apartment she had decorated made her even more eager to pinch open the top of the bag. She placed her pinky inside the bag and put some of the narcotic up to her nose. She sniffed the dope until her nose burned. She moaned from the purity of the heroin as she put her head back on the headrest, looked out the window at the falling snow, and drifted into a place where she didn't feel immediate hurt. If Alvin was determined to just get high, she vowed to get high right along with him. He complained when he thought she was just going with him for his dope. He got pissed when she begged to go for the mainline.

"Tie me off," Linda said.

He loved this woman and he knew how hard it was to get the monkey off his back. She wasn't as strong as him. He didn't wish that kind of pain on his most hated prison guard.

"You just don't understand," Alvin said as he drove faster through red lights and stop signs.

Linda was slick. She waited until Alvin was well on his way on one of his power packed trips before she asked him again to stick a needle in her arm.

"Come on baby, please. Baby, please," Linda said, holding out her bony arms as they sat in the car in Riverside Park. She had just tied him off so he could shoot dope into his vein.

"No," Alvin said as he rested his head against the window.

They stayed parked like that in Riverside Park until Alvin came back to reality. He drove off at a high rate of speed until he reached the apartment building where his sister lived. Linda was assured that she could stay with sister-in-law until she could get back on her feet. Yet the blues she felt from being forced from her 'partment clouded her thinking. She was eager to get high all of the time. Alvin pressed her about pawning the rest of her furniture to buy dope when her money ran out.

"It just ain't fair for you to get the better high," Linda said once she got Alvin's attention.

"Fair enough," Alvin said once he rolled over in the bed of his sister's spare bedroom and drifted back into reality. "If you start to feel the blues behind this shit, then that will be your fault. Don't blame me," he said. "Now, hold still."

Alvin increased Linda's dosage gradually and they got addicted together at his sister's house. When they weren't getting high they had makeup sex on the nights that Alvin wasn't chasing other women. Before long, Linda felt sick to her stomach.

She was pregnant.

Linda wasn't prepared for another child and she fretted going though what she had gone through with Tanya, always a cranky child who craved attention. Being fertile Myrtle wasn't a title that made Linda proud.

Could she take care of her new problem at the back alley clinic without Alvin finding out? She thought about sneaking to the clinic, but before her child made it to the first trimester she lost the baby. She miscarried in the bathroom after a troublesome bout of cramps.

"Oh, blood," Linda told herself the following morning and recoiled that it was only one drop of blood, like the first time she had a miscarriage. The feelings of confusion consumed her. Though inconvenient, she questioned her feelings of loss. Linda didn't know if was the dope floating through her veins, or feelings of stress brought on by the possibility that she would be forced back to her Daddy King's house, that made her lose the baby. All she knew was the baby didn't make it and it made her sad. Was it a boy, she wondered?

She never discussed the miscarriage with Alvin, whose dope habit was growing more expensive. Alvin had an insatiable appetite for the white powder. He begged, borrowed and stole for it.

Linda woke crying for three consecutive nights and kept her feelings of being depressed about her baby to herself. When Alvin pushed for sex, she told him they already had one baby to feed. She held him off until her period returned to normal. Her rejections of his sexual advances made Alvin suspicious and he accused her of fooling around. They argued so violently that they woke up the house.

"I ain't goin' keep putting up with ya'll mess," Alvin's sister said one morning over coffee. She was sick of the madness between them and worried that the police officers were clamping down on Alvin.

Her suspicions would become a reality. The Hartford detectives who showed up at her apartment were early risers. They banged on her door with force.

"You know this guy?" one detective demanded as he displayed photographs of Alvin inside a department store. "Where is he? Don't lie. We know this is your old man. Tell us now. Either way, that dirt bag is going back to jail."

Linda denied knowing Alvin's whereabouts even though he had ducked under the bed when he heard them banging on the door. She sat on the bed with her arms folded across her chest until the officers left.

"That was close," Alvin said, wiping away beads of sweat from the bridge of his nose.

"Close, huh," Linda said sarcastically.

"Yeah, close," he said. "Them pigs ain't goin' quit 'til they put me back behind bars."

"Yeah, I know."

She wished that Alvin would stay at home until his trail of unsolved burglaries went cold. But Alvin was a brazen thief when he stole to feed his drug habit. Nobody could tell him anything even if the cops were hot on his heels. The boys in blue finally caught up with Alvin during one of those nights he was racing though a speed trap. Alvin got out of the car unafraid.

"You got me," Alvin said.

Though he hadn't resisted, the officers wrestled him to the ground once the radio dispatcher announced that he was armed and dangerous.

"Dirty mothers," Alvin yelled when he fell to the ground. He was dragged inside the Morgan Street jail.

"No phone calls tonight," the desk sergeant smirked. "We have a nice cold cot here with your name posted on the bars of the cell."

Alvin slept on that cot for fourteen hours before it was time for him to appear before the Superior Court judge. The suit he wore was wrinkled and his attitude was on his face. The same judge that warned him at his previous sentencing that he was walking down a road to hell was before him. But this day, the judge was in a "let's make a deal" state of mind.

"Take the deal, Mr. Jordan," the judge said. "Take the deal."

Alvin knew that the bail commissioner had misstated his criminal record. He should have been facing three years behind bars, but the judge offered him 15 months if he waived his rights to a trial. Alvin took the deal on the spot.

There was no time for him to explain to Linda why he was headed back to Cheshire prison.

"Bye ya'll," Alvin said. "See ya later."

Linda sat in the front row, so she heard the judge and heard what Alvin had said. Yet she didn't completely understand what had happened. Had Alvin just agreed to spend another 15 months in prison?

"What they hell is going on?" she blurted out, though the court sheriffs told her to hush.

The prosecutor told the judge that Alvin had violated his probation and was up to his old ways. When the judge told Alvin he had to immediately accept or reject the deal, the public defender agreed that it was a good offer. It was normal for the judge to give a defendant time to get his or her affairs in order before being sent to prison. The judge told Alvin that if he accepted the deal, he'd be sent to prison right away.

Linda thought she could at least get to kiss him goodbye. The bailiffs surrounded her when she stood up. When she reached between them to take Alvin's hand, they pushed her back.

"Stand back, miss," a big white sheriff with a bulging belly overlapping his waistband said. "You are not allowed to touch the prisoner."

"Prisoner!" Linda said with disgust in her voice.

Her anger showed in the tears that burned down her cheeks and the piercing stare at their badges.

"Alvin, Alvin!" Linda screamed. He looked back, shook his head and mumbled to himself.

"What did he say?" Linda thought.

Before she could collect her thoughts, Alvin was yelling obscenities at the judge, his public defender and the sheriffs. "Dirty motherfuckers! Y'all shit ain't right," he yelled.

"Remove this prisoner from the courtroom," the judge, satisfied with his decision, said. "Now!"

Though he had played the role of the defeated prisoner, Alvin expected to get out on bail out that day. He was still wearing gold chains around his neck, a big fancy wristwatch and his pointy gator shoes, not the stuff he wanted to entrust to the custody of the Department of Correction. If he had had the chance, he would have stripped himself of his jewelry and expensive shoes and given them to Linda for safekeeping. If the tables had been turned, he would have pawned the stuff for a big bag of dope for himself.

"Damn," he said inside the holding cell. "They done messed up my high."

Linda stretched her neck in Alvin's direction until she saw him turn his head behind the thick metal grates. He shrugged his shoulders, showing that he had no control over the criminal justice system. In one last gesture, Alvin put his index finger and thumb to his ear letting Linda know to expect his collect telephone call.

The judge banged his gavel, alerting the sheriffs that his court was adjourned. "All rise," the sheriff announced. "Please leave the courtroom."

"Dirty motherfucker," Linda repeated Alvin's words.

"Clear the courtroom," the sheriff yelled louder. "Clear the courtroom."

Linda made such a ruckus that three burly sheriffs carried her out into the hallway. Her pretty chocolate face was streaked with tears and her pony tail attachment had come untied and had fallen on the floor.

"Here's your hair," a bailiff with a kind face said. "Calm

down. You don't want trouble."

"Trouble," Linda smirked after the bailiff put her down. She walked off murmuring toward the elevator. "You ain't seen no damn trouble. Okay."

CHAPTER 11 | PAYDAY

LINDA HAD ACTED SUCH A FOOL in the courthouse that she expected Alvin's sister would pull away the welcome mat once she returned home. But she hadn't. She was a generous host who served Linda some sweet wine to calm her nerves.

"That damn brother of mine needs his ass whupped," she said. "He knows better. He got a daughter and woman to take care."

Linda had only planned to stay with Alvin's sister in the Stowe Village Housing project until she figured out a way to get back on her feet. But days turned into lonely months. She was walking home one day when this dude from down South approached her.

"Hey, pretty lady," he said.

Linda would have raised her middle finger his way on any other day, but she hadn't had attention from a man in a while. She paused and looked back. He spoke with a slow drawl that Linda found comical. She did an about face and noticed that the man wore overalls and a flannel shirt in the summertime. His appearance made her think of country folks that came up North to share plots of land with her grandparents on the tobacco farm miles away from Hartford.

"Damn, you ain't got no style," she mumbled to herself. Once they talked for a minute, she nicknamed the kind stranger Countryman. He didn't reject the title. If he was from down South, Linda thought, he would be slow to her city ways.

"That your car?" she said. He had a beat-up Chevy.

"Yeah, it mine."

"Give me a ride?"

Countryman opened the door of his car for Linda. His toothless smile was friendly. He reminded her once more of the country people that migrated to Hartford from Alabama, Georgia and Mississippi.

"What bring you to these parts?" Linda asked as they rode slowly down the city's streets. He looked out the window with wonder, revealing that he was new to the city.

"Tobacca," he said with an easy slow drawl.

"Seem like all our people come up here to work on the farms. You from 'Bama?"

"Georgia," he said, embarrassed that the pretty dark chocolate girl was making fun of him.

Linda dated Countryman for months. He was easy on the wallet and gave her money freely for dope, diapers and milk. He also gave her money for weekend bus rides to Cheshire, for intimate visits with Alvin at the prison. All he wanted for his trouble was Linda's company. But his generosity made Linda suspicious. He wasn't down with the dope and getting high for him meant emptying a bottle of Wild Irish Rose or a bottle of cough syrup in one sitting. Countryman was afraid of the white powder Linda sniffed from tiny plastic bags she purchased for five dollars a piece. Linda used Countryman for everyday things like going to the grocery store, riding downtown and sexing it up when she needed a man's hands on her body.

Countryman loved Linda in a sweet gentle way that told her that he wasn't leaving even if she fooled around with Alvin. Countryman knew that Alvin was Linda's first love. But he didn't know to what extent until she conceived during a conjugal visit with Alvin. She turned moody and her body revealed her secret. But Countryman stayed with her nevertheless. He was with her for the long haul.

"I'm here for you," he slurred one day after he had too much wine. "I got whatever you need."

Linda thought of Countryman as a friend, but he couldn't provide the same kind of loving that she had with Alvin. He could not ignite the same sort of passionate heat that Alvin offered in the prison trailer. If Countryman wanted to stick around, so be it, Linda thought. She knew he would continue to give her money for things she needed because Alvin wasn't around to provide.

Linda's social worker allowed her to move into a two-bedroom apartment in a housing project within a mile of city hall. She was happy to move into the Martin Luther King projects on Van Block Avenue. The red brick buildings were built in 1969 in the South End of the city. Her only other alternative was to relocate to one of the remaining projects in the North End that had been spared during the race riots with police. When Alvin got out of prison, Linda established another plan to trap him into marriage.

"I'm so happy that you finally proposed," Linda said one morning after Alvin finished cleaning her apartment. Every room smelled like a mixture of Clorox and Mr. Clean. The narcotic gave Alvin energy when it made others slump, scratch and nod. The higher he got, the more Alvin cleaned.

"Propose what?" Alvin said.

Linda put her hands on her hips and sucked her teeth as she walked out of the kitchen. She revisited the subject every time Alvin spent the night. No more babies without a marriage license, Linda thought. She was determined not to have another illegitimate child. She worked on Alvin until they got a blood test and the marriage license. She was dreaming aloud about getting married when her older cousin overheard her conversation over the telephone. She was one of Linda's relatives who loved her but didn't like seeing her head down such a crooked path toward poverty. She agreed to pay for blood tests, the preacher and the license if Linda got Alvin to agree to get married before the baby was born. Linda remembered that she had promised Mommy she wouldn't be one of those young girls with lots of babies with "different mens."

"You game?" Linda asked Alvin once again.

"Game fo' what?"

"Gettin' married."

"Yeah, if you say so," Alvin said.

He was nonchalant about the subject, but Linda didn't waste time. She was five months along and her pregnancy was starting to show. She planned on wearing the white dress she had in her closet, but it was too tight and the zipper ripped apart when she tried it on. Linda borrowed a beige dress from her sister and confirmed the date. Alvin promised that he'd be at the apartment at the appointed time.

Linda cleaned up like she was expecting company for the rest of the week. But she wasn't as sentimental about her new place as she had been about her first apartment. The kitchen was sparsely decorated with a table, two chairs and a high chair for Tanya. She had a sofa and coffee table in the living room, a twin bed in her bedroom and a crib in the second bedroom.

Everyone she invited showed up the following Saturday. The apartment was buzzing with her relatives when someone knocked on the door.

"Who's that white man?" Linda asked.

"He ain't white. Spanish," her cousin offered. "Open the door. That's the justice of the peace."

Two hours passed when Alvin finally showed up with his best friend. "What's going on? Ya'll started the party without me?" Alvin said.

"We gettin' married," Linda said.

"Oh, yeah," Alvin slurred.

He was high, but nothing was going to stop Linda from getting married to him. She ordered Alvin to put on a suit jacket.

"Where you been?" Linda asked.

"New York," Alvin said.

Linda ushered her family and friends into the living room where the minister, a short bookish-looking Puerto Rican, sat patiently on the couch reading from his Bible.

"We ready," she said.

Linda and Alvin stood before the man and listened closely as he read from the Bible. The ceremony was comical to both of them. The preacher hardly spoke English and his words were barely recognizable. Linda and Alvin eyed one another and giggled.

"You kiss the bride," the preacher man said and puckered his lips.

That's when Linda slapped the spit out of Alvin's mouth.

"Blam! I got ya now!" Linda screamed. Their families perked up to see what she'd do next.

Though Alvin was her first love, Linda hadn't forgotten how he raped her when she was ten years old. She promised herself for the following decades, especially during the difficult times when Alvin was in prison, that he would pay for making her raise Tanya by herself. He was going to be a husband and a father whether he liked it or not.

"I got ya now," she repeated slowly.

Her words stung like the swelling in Alvin's mouth. Linda expected him to slap her down, but he backed away, looking puzzled and dazed. The minister also hadn't expected Linda's violent outburst. He quickly packed up his Bible, mumbled congratulations and left the apartment.

Somebody opened the refrigerator after the ceremony and it became clear that Linda and Alvin had not planned a reception. There was nothing to eat or drink. There was only one ice tray in the fridge.

"Y'all ain't got no food," one of Linda's sisters yelled into the living room. "How we gonna have a wedding reception without no food. I'm hungry and thirsty too."

Linda's uncles from her mother's side of the family stepped up before she could explain. One passed his Stetson around the living room and collected enough money for several buckets of Kentucky Fried Chicken. Alvin reached into his wallet and pulled out enough money for a gallon of gin and a few fifths of wine. He pointed to the door when somebody mentioned that there was no beer in the house. "Get it ya damn self."

The family partied well into the night. Those who didn't get drunk got high. Emotions were just as high when Linda walked in on her older sister, who was having an argument with her man. They were about to go to blows when Linda sucker-punched her sister's man. Alvin had followed behind Linda and before they knew it, both couples were tussling on the floor in the kitchen. A neighbor heard the commotion through the paper-thin walls and called the police, who hauled them all to jail for drinking and fighting. Everyone but Alvin was released that night. The arraignment judge read the police report, which contained pertinent details about his criminal history, and concluded that Alvin had violated the conditions of his parole. He was headed back to prison.

Linda was five months pregnant that night on July 5, 1974, and happy about being married. She had kept her promise to Mommy.

Linda refused to go back to St. Francis, a Catholic hospital, when her time came to have the baby. Though she hated the clinic and McCook Public Hospital, she had heard that the staff at St. Francis would save the baby before saving the mother's life. She didn't want to risk dying during delivery and realized that she had made the right choice.

The baby she would name Tasha was an easy pregnancy but a troubling delivery. She weighed 6 pounds and 5 ounces, a big baby for a woman of Linda's size.

"I done had another girl," she wrote in her letters to Alvin. Tasha, a beautiful chocolate baby, looked like both of them, she said.

"A baby, huh. How you gonna feed it with me in here?" Alvin wrote back.

Linda thought a new baby would pull Alvin out of his funky mood. The tone of his letters had been ornery and smart-mouthed since his mother died. His grief was exacerbated years before when he was forced to attend the funeral in Hartford in chains. Linda had noticed that Alvin wasn't his old cocky self when the prison guards ushered him into the service. Alvin ignored the pain of his loss while in prison, but now his pain was all over his face as he bent to inspect his mother's face inside the casket.

"I feel for him," Linda told Auntie as they watched Alvin shuffling in the leg irons. "I wanna hold him and wipe the tears that I knows he won't let fall from his eyes. I think maybe one day he'll stop doing them drugs and my love be all he need."

Linda had those reoccurring feelings since the first time Alvin was sent away. When he walked past her at the service he gave her attitude, and it set her off.

"I should'a known he wasn't going to change," Linda told her Auntie. "He always talking me into splitting my state check with him, so he can buy some squares to share with his cellie."

Linda heard later, from the women gossiping on the bus to the prison, that Alvin sold jailhouse hooch. He always had money hidden in his mattress during the prison inspections. She knew then that Alvin was playing the same game on her, taking her money, as she had with Countryman.

Linda's dreams about encouraging Alvin to stay clean faded once he was released from prison after Tasha's birth. She had a heroin jones of her own each time she and her Auntie Mary, one of her mother's ten siblings, shared a bag of dope on the weekends before they made it over to her Grandma P's Saturday night card parties in the Square. Linda had promised herself that she wouldn't get heroin sick, but the narcotics had imprisoned her mind.

"It feel like morning sickness and monthly cramps rolling around my belly," Linda told Countryman during a weak moment. "Damn, I'm hooked on that dope."

Countryman nodded when she told him. "Can I help?"

"Nope," she said, her voice trailing off.

Countryman was good about giving Linda money when she needed it. She felt bad about cheating on Alvin with Countryman, because she was still sleeping from time to time at Alvin's sister's house when she wanted to be closer to the dope man. She drifted back to her family to ease her guilt. Her aunt and sister kept Tanya most of the time anyway. They let Linda and the new baby stay for a few nights, before she convinced the social worker that she was responsible enough to get an apartment in the same red brick projects where her sister lived.

"I'll be all right," she thought.

Linda was fixing her sister's hair one day when the subject of her relationship with Countryman came up. "He don't seem like the kind of man you fools with," her sister said.

"I know, huh. He act like he knows what goes on in the streets," Linda laughed. "I play it off. If he wanna be in the game, he gonna get played. He always got cash in his pockets. I picked them with my charm, always smiling and throwing kisses his way. He was too stupid to figure out he'll have to work a lot harder to stay closer to my pootang. He claims he is down with the dope thang. But every time he come back with a bag for me, he buys Wild Irish Rose for himself. He claim it get him higher than dope do. Yeah, right.

"I tell you what I do know. Anything them babies need, Pampers, milk or clothes, he drives me to get it and buys it, too. I didn't feel nothin' when we finally kicked off some sex. He don't look nor smell nothing like my Alvin. He didn't have that same sense of style as that crooked black man of mine."

Countryman had helped Linda when it came time for her to move into her next apartment. She didn't have the money or the energy to fix it up like her first apartment. She settled for twin beds, some sheets and towels the social worker offered her. Once she got back on her feet, Linda walked with confidence, and other men noticed the young mother who carried one baby on her hip and pushed the other one in a stroller. She was carrying groceries inside one day when a new man in town rolled down the window of his shiny Chevy and whistled at her.

"Damn baby, you sho' is fine. Sweet as a Hershey bar," he said. "I'm gonna make you one of mine."

"One of yours," Linda blushed and smiled. "What you mean by that."

"Wanna find out?" said the man. He wore a bright red polyester suit with a royal blue trim. "They call me Knight."

Before Linda knew it, the stranger was treating her better than Countryman. She accepted his generosity when he offered to take her to the beauty shop and to buy her clothes from the department stores downtown. She was sweet on him until he told her that he didn't like kids. Linda schemed to get as much as she could from Knight, until he got possessive.

Things got worse when her new friend saw her walking down the street talking to another man who was trying to turn her on to a new brand of heroin. Linda was smiling a little too much when she met back up with Knight at her apartment.

"Trying to give away my stuff?" he yelled.

"Say what?" Linda said. She quickly backed off when Knight gave her a look that might drop kick her dead.

Smooth this over, Linda thought. She was a known fighter but she wasn't stupid, so she smiled. Before she could say another word, Knight, who towered over her, belted her in the mouth. His blows were so hard that Linda didn't have the strength to fight back. She yelped and whimpered each time he hit her.

Knight was exhausted after he beat her up. He passed out cold after he stole her precious jewels on the bed. Her mouth was bloody and she thought she had lost all her teeth until she looked in the mirror. Her face was swollen, her eyes were black, and her mouth looked and felt worse than any extraction at the dentist. Linda knew he would kill her if she stayed there until morning. She ran for the door, and took off running with only the clothes on her back. She ended up at Daddy Harry's door in the wee hours of the morning. Though she didn't spend a lot of time with her real Daddy, she knew he cared for her and could protect her in ways that no other man had.

Daddy Harry greeted Knight at the door holding his Smith and Wesson. "You got forty-eight hours to get out of town," Daddy Harry warned.

The expression on the man's face looked as dead as the roses he had purchased for Linda at the corner store. He stayed away. Linda was happy when she heard the stranger got busted for trying to kill somebody else's woman. Linda left Daddy Harry's house after she promised him that she would stay away from brutes like that. "Come to me if you need something," he said.

Linda was desperate when she returned to her apartment. Her first instinct was to move, but her social worker refused to accept her calls. Linda found comfort in the only way she knew how. She sold her food stamps and cashed her government checks. Her heroin habit was firmly on her back by then. She hardly came out her bedroom where she kept her works: used needles, a candle, a bottle cap and a bottle of bleach to clean her needles. Countryman didn't ask any questions when she threatened "to leave his sorry ass" if he didn't give her money for the dope she craved. She knew he felt sorry for her. Tanya was growing fast and Tasha was always hungry. Linda couldn't remember when her oldest child started walking. She had missed a lot.

When Linda was high, she daydreamed about her mother before she lapsed into a coma when her liver failed. Mommy was an evil woman sometimes, and her anger was relentless toward anyone in her way. Linda flinched when she thought about the day Mommy was giving Tanya a beating for standing up in the bathtub. She burst into the bathroom and jumped in to protect her daughter.

"Step back," Mommy yelled. "This got to be done. Somebody got to teach this chile some manners. I won't allow this gal to talk to me any ol' kind of way."

Mommy drew her arm back and gave Tanya another lashing when Linda screamed in her defense. Though she beat Tanya regularly, Linda didn't want anyone else putting his or her hands on her child. She reached for the baby, and Mommy threw a pot of boiling water that was by the tub at her. The water, boiled because the apartment was out of hot water, splashed all over Linda's chest and arms, making her yell loud enough to wake Jesus. The neighbors heard the noise and called the police.

Linda was in the kitchen nursing her wounds when a police officer sat down next to her at the kitchen table.

"Tell me," the police officer said.

Linda made up a story about getting burnt when she dropped a pot of water on the stove. The officer wasn't convinced. He reported a 10-10, the police department's code for an ambulance, and questioned Linda repeatedly about the incident. But Linda kept to her story. She knew how embarrassing it would be for the family if the authorities knew they didn't have hot water in the bathroom and boiled water on a gas burner for their baths. The scars on her arms and chest healed slowly, constantly reminding Linda of Mommy's scalding hot temper. She healed her internal wounds on the weekends when she shared needles filled with heroin.

Mommy died without knowing that Linda was using dope to medicate herself from the pain of those kinds of memories. When Linda came home sleepy and tired, Mommy assumed that Linda had turned into an alcoholic. On good nights, she shared a few drinks with her to calm the troubling waters rising up between them. Mommy was buried in a grave without a headstone.

On this day, Linda fixed herself up because it was time to visit the social worker, who controlled the food stamps and checks. Linda picked out a long- sleeved shirt to cover the track marks on her arms forming like pimples around her veins. She combed her hair straight back and slicked it down with grease until it reached the nape of her neck, before tying it tight with a rubber band and attaching a long wavy hair piece to her ponytail. She rubbed Vaseline all over her face and massaged the burns on her chest, her elbows and knees until the ashy dry spots were covered by a petroleum shine.

She had another reason to leave her bedroom, her private dope den, to look good. Alvin had made parole. He had been home for a few days before he visited Linda. He noticed that Countryman was still hanging around Linda like a stray puppy that put up with more than he deserved.

"Who this?" Alvin asked.

"Just a friend of the family," Linda said. "Good people."

"If you gonna hang around here, you need to give me the same type of funds you is giving Linda," Alvin said. "That your ride outside?"

Countryman nodded, not sure what to do or say.

"Let me take her for a spin," Alvin said.

Countryman was unaware of what he was up against. He handed Alvin the keys to his car and the mileage that Alvin put on his car racked up quickly. Alvin was making runs to Harlem for heroin to sell in Hartford.

Countryman loved Linda. His head was in the clouds over the Hershey chocolate-toned girl. He felt used by Alvin, but never questioned him when he demanded his keys and gas money. Linda shook her head in disgust when she found out that Alvin was playing games with Countryman.

"You been using his car?" Linda asked Alvin.

"Yep."

"What he thinking? That's one weak-minded man," she laughed. "You can't respect mens like that. Love is one thing. But he actin' stupid."

"What you care?" Alvin asked when Linda stayed on the subject longer than he thought she should.

"Care? He ain't my problem," Linda said.

Alvin continued to use Countryman's car as if it were his own, and Linda rode Countryman for every dime he could spare. Over time, Alvin came to like Countryman, even if he wasn't wise about the ways of the street. One Saturday, Alvin convinced Countryman to ride with him to New York because he didn't want to get stopped by state police for driving without a license.

"Yeah, I can do that," Countryman said.

They were at a toll booth on the New York State Thruway later that day when a state trooper rode up behind them. The trooper waited for them to make it through the booth when he turned on his siren and stopped the car.

"Let me handle them," Alvin told Countryman.

Countryman rolled down the window when the trooper approached them. He volunteered that it was his car. He also volunteered to the trooper that they were leaving New York and were heading back to Hartford.

"Long day," the trooper asked. "Did you know your tail light was out?"

"Yes sir," said Countryman.

Countryman accepted the ticket. He grinned at the trooper, hoping that he wouldn't ask to search the car. Alvin had installed a secret place inside the glove compartment and behind the eight-track player to conceal his heroin and contraband. Countryman had discovered the hiding places when he popped out a Curtis Mayfield tape from the player and packets of heroin popped out onto the floor.

Alvin sulked throughout their ride home. When Country-man pulled the car over at Linda's place, Alvin tried beating the crap out of Countryman, but he was too high to give him a prop-er beating. He walked into the house calling Linda's name.

"Let me tell you bout this nigga of yours. We got stopped by a state trooper in his raggedy-ass car. I told him from the get-go to let me do the talking. But he volunteered where we had been and where we were going. I told the motherfucker before we stopped to keep his motherfucking mouth shut. Does he do it?" Alvin said, "Nah, he just kept talking."

Countryman was still smarting over the incident the following day. When Alvin opened the door, he pulled out a rusty knife and tried sticking Alvin with it.

"You a murderer now?" Alvin said sarcastically. He took the knife away from Countryman and taunted him with his words. "What you gonna do? Cut me? Take your sorry ass back to Alabama, Mississippi or Georgia, or wherever the fuck you from."

Countryman walked away without saying goodbye. He knew he was no match for Alvin, who had taught him about the ways of the streets. Countryman knew that Alvin was capable of killing him, but he was grateful that he had let him walk away.

Alvin had other things on his mind. His regular customers were coming over to the house but he had used more dope from his package from New York than he was selling. Dope was sparse in Hartford. Alvin thought it was time to implement the scheme he told Linda about.

"You know them bank deposit slips they give you at the bank," Alvin said. "Some old white dude dropped one of his in the bank. I picked it up."

He could hardly read the Polish man's name when he went to his connection and got his photograph taken with the stranger's name printed on a new state identification card. Once he got the card, he returned to the bank wearing a nice suit and picked out the youngest bank teller to wait on him. He told the man that he had been ripped off and needed new checks. The bank manager was too green to ask the right questions. Alvin walked out carrying temporary checks with the old man's name on them.

Alvin revealed his plan to Linda because he knew she was sweet on Countryman. If she charmed him back into her good graces, Alvin thought she could talk Countryman into letting Alvin use his car until he cashed enough checks to buy a new car of his own.

"If my boy's car was running I wouldn't come to you," Alvin said. "Let's ride, nigga?"

"Nah, he always comes through for me," Linda said. "When you need the car?"

"Tomorrow," Alvin said.

"Done."

Alvin hit a bank every day for a week using Countryman's car. He would have kept using it, but the old jalopy was unreliable. He needed a car that would take him from Hartford, down state and up into Massachusetts and Rhode Island in one day. The old man's name and his bank account had paid off like a bookie's receipts. Once Alvin got home, he had cash and dope that he shared with Linda. But she always wanted more.

"Where the groceries?" Linda asked.

"Hurry up. It's time to get high," Alvin told her after he pulled his car up to her door. "Let's go."

Alvin rolled up to the curb of the grocery store and Linda got out. Alvin caught up with Linda and grabbed the cart. He pushed the buggy through the aisles like a speed demon, tossing food he craved while he was in prison from the shelves. Linda was more frugal and put some of the food back on the shelves when Alvin turned his back.

Their dance went on until the twenty-six thousand dollars Alvin had stolen from the elderly Polish man was spent. While Linda liked the steady flow of cash, she was afraid that Alvin would get caught and she would be sandwiched in the middle of his deception with the police. Her worst fear was that she'd get arrested right along with Alvin, and she'd have to go toe to toe with some big burly woman at Niantic, the women's prison.

Linda thought it was just her nerves when she started getting sick to her stomach every time she smelled food. She thought for a moment that it might have been a side effect of the dope, but deep down she knew the truth. She was pregnant again. But this time, she was married.

She didn't bank on Alvin going back to prison. She decided to try fending for herself. She cleaned offices in the insurance companies up the street on nights she could. It was not easy to find a babysitter in the South End of Hartford, because she was a North side girl. Having the extra cash helped on days she felt the stomach cramps from her heroin jones. The cash helped more than the food stamps and check from The Welfare. She wasn't rolling in dough but she wasn't hurting either. The rent was paid and food was in the refrigerator.

Alvin had trouble with the law before the wedding. It seemed like the cops were always stopping him for this and that, mostly for driving unregistered cars. He would pay a fine and get released on minor motor vehicle charges. Alvin didn't understand the concept of paying for a license, insurance and taxes before he got behind the wheel. He figured if he could get the car, he should be allowed to drive it.

"It's my car. I don't need no registration," Alvin argued when Linda bailed him out of jail.

The police and the FBI were also after him for selling and using drugs and were following up on an anonymous tip that he had been cashing illegal checks. But Alvin was one of those slick criminals who eluded the law for years after he finished serving time for violating his parole. The cops had him under surveillance when he exited a bar on The Avenue carrying an album cover that he used to conceal packets of heroin he sold on the side. Inside the bar he had sold a ten-dollar bag to a man who would turn out to be an undercover agent. He was strolling down the street when he spotted two detectives walking up behind him.

"What you got?" the detectives asked.

"What I got? What you mean?"

The officers slapped each other on the backs and plastered sly smiles on their faces. "Everything is on tape. We got you, boy," one of the officers said.

"Boy," Alvin responded. "I got your boy. Why ya'll messing with me?"

Alvin was seasoned at this banter. He didn't volunteer any information. He just smiled. The next thing he knew, police cars were racing down the street toward the curb where he was standing.

Alvin gave all the uniformed and plainclothes cops an "I'm ain't worried" look. He took on the posture of a bad dude, a "try something and you might get something" persona. He was ready to fight for his freedom until six or eight police officers pinned him against a parked car.

"What I do?"

"You'll find out," said one police officer who had arrested Alvin before. "Remember me?"

"Yeah, I remember. What now?"

The officers told Alvin that he had been caught selling dope to an undercover agent. He was cold busted, the officers roared in unison as they wielded billy clubs at his legs.

"Wait a minute, wait a minute," Alvin yelled.

The officers had their hands all over him. They patted him down and reached down his pants.

"Y'all ain't got to do all that. I wasn't holding nothing but that there album cover. Did you look at it? Smokey Robinson and the Miracles, you heard of them?"

The officers ignored Alvin and pulled him inside the black and white cruiser. Alvin smiled. He learned long ago that the police expect suspects to lie. They don't expect a career criminal to willingly point them in the direction of the proof they needed for probable cause. Alvin had tricked them. They left Smokey's songs on the ground with fifty dollars worth of dope tucked inside.

The police dragged Alvin into the police station. He wasn't giving them an inch of cooperation and his outbursts caused other officers to surround him carrying their clubs. They had handcuffed his hands behind his back and tied his ankles together with rope. All Alvin had to fight back with was his words. He had hated the police since he was a kid. They always jacking me and my boys up, Alvin thought.

"I want a damn lawyer. This here is police brutality," he yelled.

The officers placed Alvin in a dingy dark cell with a toilet that smelled like it was backing up. He sucked in the smell of urine and bowel for another two hours before a "narco" hit the iron bars with his handcuffs.

"Get over here," he said.

"You talking to me?" Alvin said as he strutted toward the bars. "What you want?"

The short, stubby undercover officer had shoulder length hair and razor cuts tattooed on his face. "Shut up and listen. You ain't getting out of this one," he whispered. "That cat wearing the big yellow suit on the corner bar stool wasn't a dope fiend. He was one of us and he caught you on the wire."

Now ain't that a bitch, Alvin mumbled to himself. "When ya'll start hiring black police?" Once he knew what the detectives were up to, Alvin kept his cards close and refused to answer any questions when he was placed in the interrogation room. But he had a few pertinent questions of his own.

"Y'all got any tea? Any Kool-Aid? What y'all be drinking up in here besides coffee? Give me one of them cigarettes."

The interrogation went on for hours before Alvin remembered that he had given Linda some cash to hold. Maybe she'll bail him out, he thought, knowing that she wouldn't be happy once she learned that he would be spending the night in a new bed in a dingy cell.

"Can I get my phone call?"

The two plainclothes officers ignored Alvin's requests and

peppered him with questions. When he asked one too many times for a lawyer, the men sat back in their chairs and gave Alvin the silent treatment. One of them rubbed his bald head, and the other man smirked.

"Aw shit, man. I got rights, too."

The detectives were stalling for a reason. They had been trailing Alvin for the past week and recording his every move in their spiral notebooks. On the day of the bust, city police and federal agents hooked up a reel-to-reel tape player behind the bar. While he sipped beer and sold heroin, they recorded his conversations, and relished the thought that Alvin Jordan would once again be wearing his inmate number sewn across a prison uniform.

When Alvin got to court the following day, he had stale breath and sleep in his eyes. His Afro was uncombed and his clothes were wrinkled. He immediately recognized that he had been in the company of the prosecutor and the judge before. They were whispering on the side of the bench when he stood behind the defendant's table next to the unorganized public defender rifling though his papers.

"Your honor, the state is dropping the charges," the prosecutor announced. "The U.S. Attorney of Connecticut will be prosecuting Mr. Jordan as an interstate drug trafficker who runs drugs from New York to Hartford. This case is going federal."

"Federal!" Alvin yelled. "This is some bullshit."

"Quiet. Quiet in the courtroom," the bailiff said.

"He's facing at least 10 to 20 years," the prosecutor continued. Alvin was dumbstruck.

The public defender took off his bifocals and leaned over to talk to Alvin, who was wiggling his hands in the handcuffs.

"Plead guilty," the government-paid lawyer said. "Right now! Tell the judge you are guilty and that you are prepared to serve five years."

"If they want me locked up for another 20 years, they goin' to have to take me to trial," Alvin said. "That's what you should be telling that damn judge. Shut up! Fuck you! Fuck all ya'll." Alvin yelled so loudly that court bailiffs ran into the courtroom from all directions. The judge, who wasn't in any mood to argue, slammed his gavel down.

"Get him out of here," the judge said as four husky bailiffs dragged Alvin back into the cage.

Later, when Alvin got back to the penitentiary, he laughed aloud to himself because he had not been arrested for cashing illegal checks.

"What's so funny?" his cellmate asked, looking up at Alvin from the bottom bunk.

"I stole, stole big time," Alvin bragged. "My plan worked. I went to the bank and waited until some dumb ass white dude, who was slow, crippled and clumsy, dropped his deposit slip at my feet. His name, account number and balance were printed on the slip. I looked at that old man as he walked slowly out of the bank. He had given me a something big, a twenty six thousand dollar gift. From then on, I quit the garage. Working that bank account became my new job."

"Damn, man, what happened next?" Alvin's new cellmate, a big muscled convict, asked.

"I'll tell you the rest later. I'm going to sleep."

A FAMILY PORTRAIT

1. Harry Hartie, of
Hartford, was Linda's
biological father. She
didn't get to know
him until she became
a single-mother at
age 16. Harry is a
community activist in
Hartford.

2. Linda's mother
Edith Parkman
Shannon died
when she was
young woman.

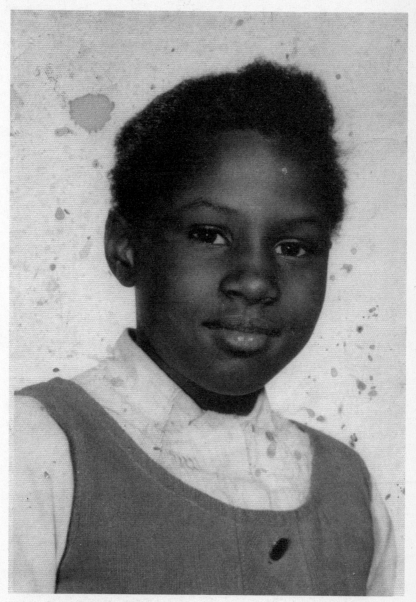

3. Linda was a school girl in this picture. Hartie kept it as a keepsake at his home in Hartford.

4. Photograph from Aids prevention poster.

5. Homecoming. Alvin gets out of prison.

5. Linda gets her children out of foster care and also a new home in West Hartford.

5. Linda's father, King Shannon

CHAPTER 12 | DOWNFALL

LINDA WAS WRESTLING WITH A BAD DREAM when the telephone rang before daybreak. She didn't feel like answering it. But six-year-old Tanya had crawled up on her bed and cried each time she heard the loud clanging ring.

"Mommy, the phone," Tanya whined.

"Let it ring," Linda yelled. "I'm trying to get some sleep." She was nursing a hangover and wasn't in the mood to talk to anybody.

But the caller was persistent.

"What is it!" Linda yelled into the receiver.

"Alvin is locked up," her sister-in-law said.

"What?"

Linda sat up. She listened as Alvin's sister explained that the neighborhood was buzzing about how a gang of police officers dragged Alvin down The Avenue in the back of a police car. He had fought back and they beat him up pretty badly, his sister said. She said she called the police station throughout the night but hadn't gotten anywhere with the desk sergeant.

"Where he at?" Linda asked.

"I don't know."

Linda hung up the telephone and put a pillow over her head, hoping her headache would go away. She knew she had to get up. The social worker from Tanya's school would check whether she was in kindergarten. Thoughts of being reported to The Welfare for child neglect nagged at her, but Linda didn't feel like getting out of bed. The depression kept her in bed for another hour.

Linda didn't answer the telephone when it rang again, but she got up. She forced Tanya into the bathroom and washed her face, hands and bottom with a face cloth. She placed a bowl of generic cereal and drenched it in watered-down powdered milk while Tanya watched cartoons on TV.

"Eat this," Linda yelled.

When Tanya refused to move, Linda got angrier.

"Move!"

Tired and blue, Linda convinced herself that she could lie down. She tossed and turned until Alvin's sister called again. Alvin was at the Morgan Street jail and probably wouldn't be home again for another three or four years. The police had caught him selling heroin.

Linda slammed down the telephone and paced the floors of her apartment. She could no longer depend on that damn jailbird, Linda thought, when she heard someone banging on the front door. She scanned her apartment. Heaps of dirty laundry littered the floors. Bowls of spoiled milk filled the kitchen sink. There were empty rum bottles on the table and the garbage reeked of spoiled food in a grease-stained paper grocery bag on the floor. She didn't want to open the door, but the banging wouldn't stop.

"Who the hell is it?" Linda yelled.

"Miss Mack. Can I come in?"

There was no way Linda was going to let the social worker inside her place in this condition.

"We all got colds," Linda lied as she cracked opened the door. "Can you come back another time?"

The aging social worker feared contagious diseases and backed away from the door. "Call me," she said.

Linda had hated cleaning since she was a child. But she knew that Miss Mack was good at her job. She would be back to check on the girls. She scrubbed down her apartment and took out the garbage. She washed loads of clothes and hung them to dry on chairs in the kitchen and on radiators throughout the apartment. The smell of the bleach that she used to mop the kitchen, bathroom and bedrooms floors for the next few hours cleared her head long enough for her to remember she had hidden a hit of dope in her bureau. She was tempted to drift back into her bedroom, but thoughts of Miss Mack reminded her that her girls hadn't eaten a decent meal in days.

Linda picked out one of her last two boxes of elbow macaroni from the kitchen cabinet. She boiled the noodles in water, heated powdered milk and cheddar cheese on the stove and used the last of the dried milk to make a bottle for Tasha. Her girls were happy and their bellies were full. Linda felt satisfied that she had done her job as a parent during a weak moment.

She fought off her craving and settled for the rum she found in a kitchen cabinet. She poured herself a glass once the girls settled back in front of the TV. She thought about her limited options at the kitchen table. She lit her last Kool cigarette and considered what she had to work with. She had a two-bedroom apartment with a full basement. Daddy Harry loved her and had proved repeatedly that he was there for her despite her addictions. Though her girls got on her nerves, they loved her, too. Her worker hadn't cut off her checks and food stamps, and then there was Alvin. She reached for the empty package of Kools.

"Damn," Linda cursed as she searched the ashtray for a butt that was long enough to light. "Shit, shit, shit. I need some air!"

Linda looked in on the girls, whose eyes were glued to the television set. She walked outside into the courtyard. She saw Thelma, one of the few friends in the Martin Luther King projects, hanging laundry.

"Could I get a square?"

Thelma looked at Linda and smiled. She wasn't sure what to say when she saw Linda walking aimlessly around the courtyard. Her nightgown was stained and dirty, and her hair was all over her head. Linda's smile mirrored what Thelma felt when she noticed her friend walking in her direction. She looked helpless but determined.

"I gotta ... I gotta find a way to take care of my girls," Linda said as tears filled her eyes.

"Any young woman with a little girl and a baby in diapers feels like you do sometimes," Thelma consoled.

Linda paced around the yard in slow deliberate steps until her friend held out a cigarette. Linda took it and broke down before she could light it. Her friend was older and wiser and recognized the hurt in Linda's eyes. Linda reached out to Thelma. She cried and moaned in her friend's arms until the tears stopped coming.

"Alvin is locked up," Linda said.

"I heard," Thelma said. "What you gonna do now?"

"That's what I'm trying to figure out," Linda admitted. "That question been in my head since Alvin's sister called to tell me that he was locked down. It ain't like he been here for me for years. Seem like them cops been on his tail since he got out. I don't know. But I gots to do somethang. All I can think about is getting more work. I can clean those office buildings at them insurance companies up the street, but I ain't got nobody regular to watch the girls."

"Times like these are hard," Thelma said. "What you gonna do?"

"I don't know," Linda said.

"Think, chile. Think."

Thelma handed Linda another cigarette and she smoked it to the end of the butt.

"I can do hair, fry chicken and clean," Linda said of the skills she learned before she left home.

There were enough women in the Kings who did hair, so that wasn't an option. When Linda mentioned her famous fried chicken, Thelma had an epiphany.

"You could sell them dinners. Maybe we could start having card parties on the weekends and you could sell dinners like the churches do," Thelma said. "That could bring extra money. The

Welfare people won't find out if you don't disturb Miss Mary. Invite the rest of our nosy neighbors so they don't feel left out."

"Sounds good," Linda said, and perked up.

"Miss Mary won't bother us if I send her a plate," Linda said, thinking of the older woman next door. "I don't play cards but I know lots of people who do. If I charge at the door, I can pay for all the extra things I need and want. Okay!"

Linda left the yard feeling better. She and Thelma agreed to wait until the first of the month to hold the parties because both of them would have money. Once her food stamps came in the mail, Linda sold half of her food stamps to buy paint and decorative lights for the basement. Thelma brought over card tables and metal chairs she bought at the thrift store. They lined them up in rows of three on the concrete basement floor, and they visualized the upcoming parties. Linda kept so busy that she didn't think much about getting high, but she drank beer and rum that she had purchased for the card parties.

"You found somebody to paint yet?" Thelma asked.

"Nah," Linda said. "I'm not ready to have no strange mens hanging around."

"Who you 'spect gonna be at them card parties?"

"Strange mens," Linda laughed.

It was 1976, a good time for black folks who liked to dance in Hartford. House parties were raging throughout the city and Linda was ready to cash in. Linda envisioned ways to fix up her basement each time she tipped out at night to a party once she put her girls to sleep. She liked the red, yellow and blue strobe lights, the burning candles on card tables, and the funky style the walls were painted at other house parties. Her record player was old but it would do, Linda thought. Thelma recommended that they bring Jack and Tiptoe, two men who did odd jobs around the Kings, as partners.

Word quickly spread around the King projects. Jack and Tiptoe were ready to work once Linda called them. They took the blue, yellow, red and green paint she brought and painted every brick on the basement walls a different color. They transformed Linda's basement into the neighborhood speakeasy and card joint. They were excited about the parties and chipped in twenty-five dollars each to pay for food and liquor.

"I can work the front door," Jack said during a pre-party meeting at Linda's kitchen table.

"I can work the back," Tiptoe volunteered.

"Bouncers," Linda said. "If y'all charge a dollar or two for the folks who wanna come, we can make our money back."

A laid-off bartender helped serve beer and liquor behind the bar. Linda served fried chicken sandwiches on Wonder bread and charged two dollars. The guys charged a fee at the front and back doors. Tiptoe, a sharp dresser and a playboy, was known favorably among people in Hartford. He spread the word about the parties on the weekends at Linda's apartment at 97D Van Block Avenue in the Kings. His contacts helped Linda establish a regular clientele in the South Side. Those who lived in the Kings and other public housing projects, Dutch Point, Charter Oak, Coast Garden and Sheldon Oak, came in droves, especially during the first of the month when people received their checks. They laughed, cracked on bad players and hosted energetic games anytime somebody won a big hand playing spades or got bent out of shape during a game of bid whist. The card players had to pay the house five dollars a hand and they were lined up to play winners.

It began as good clean fun. By daylight on Saturday mornings, Linda and her crew kicked the hardcore players out of the house, paid one another and saved money for the house to restock the beer, the liquor and the food for the following weekend. Linda drank herself to sleep during the rest of the week. She dreamed of providing a hip place where people could enjoy themselves without worrying about getting into trouble. Linda made a good choice in selecting Jack and Tiptoe as her bouncers. They flexed their muscles when necessary and raised their voices when any-one resisted being frisked at the door.

"No guns, knives or vendettas," they would say. "Keep that kind of mess outside."

Linda was strict about enforcing the house rules. She didn't want anyone shot, cut or beat up attending her parties. She also didn't want anyone getting high in her basement, but if they showed up high, that was okay. Trouble stayed away from most of Linda's basement card parties. Disgruntled men or women standing outside nursing their wounds were invited inside the kitchen, where she treated them to her famous fried chicken and helped them nurse their broken hearts. Linda was proud about talking a battered woman out of confronting her lying, cheating man. It was a sermon Linda preached with authority because Alvin, her trouble man, was behind bars.

"Ain't no man worth all that," Linda would say as the woman

nodded in agreement.

Linda liked dancing. The music was usually loud enough for her to hear it when she was cooking and serving meals in the kitchen. If she didn't hear the crowd responding to the grooves of her favorite crooners or chanting "party in the house," Linda tiptoed disapprovingly down into the basement and grabbed the hand of an available man so they could restart the party. Linda hated a stale party. She didn't want that kind of reputation.

"We don't 'llow no wallflowers in my set," Linda laughed as she popped her fingers and twisted her hips. Her enthusiasm was as infectious as a honeybee. Before she knew it, people were placing their cards face down on tables and getting up on the tiny dance floor. Her energy eased any tensions when players were getting too serious at the card tables.

Grandma P taught Linda how to entertain during childhood when she hosted cookouts and card parties in the Square. Linda initially outlawed gambling at her parties. But once she saw money being passed around on the tables, she called her team together and they agreed that if any table played for money, the card players had to pay twenty dollars to the house. Nobody complained about the high-stakes games that went on well into the morning, and Linda made bacon and egg breakfasts for the diehard card players. The gamblers who had money left paid two dollars for a meal.

"I gotta eat, too," Linda told them when they balked at the cost for eggs and bacon.

The high rollers were usually drug dealers who would sneak tiny bags of dope into Linda's basement. Linda found out one night while watching a game. Every time the table bet a hand of cards, a player would slip the tiny package of dope under the stacks of money on the table. Linda had a weakness for the "White Horse," a popular nickname for the narcotic, so she didn't freak out. She quietly pulled aside a dealer at one of the tables during a break to let him know that she was hip to the real game. He offered to give Linda a taste of the narcotic the Vietnam vets had been bragging about.

She invited the dealer into her laundry room and they shared needles. Before that first time, Linda and her posse had slipped once or twice during a party, but mostly they stayed away from the white powder that first year. Linda was a born addict. Her appetite for heroin grew out of control and she turned her head when the dealers took control. She lost her focus about why she was having the parties in the first place.

Once heroin became a fixture at the basement parties, her regular customers who were hardworking card players relinquished their seats to hardcore junkies and drug dealers. Linda got afraid that the police had planted a snitch, so when a dealer got busted outside her door, she passed the word that she was taking a break.

"I'm tired," she lied.

The straight card players got the hint and they stopped coming. Linda's basement quickly became a haven for dealers, folks who occasionally sniffed the narcotic and hardcore intravenous mainline users like her.

Linda relied on her cousins and good friends to watch her daughters, Tanya and Tasha, during the parties in the basement.

But even they were scared away when the scene changed. Linda gave the girls loose change and candy to keep them quiet.

"Stay upstairs," Linda told the girls when they got curious. She was grateful that none of the men got fresh with the girls when she wasn't watching.

Linda made sure that the junkies took their needles home with them or gave them to somebody to hold when they didn't have a regular place to stay. She had no problem allowing strange men and women to camp out on her living room sofa and on the floor after the parties, especially if they shared their dope or cash with her. The foot traffic leading up to Linda's apartment was steady during the wee hours of the night and her neighbors noticed that a new kind of party was going on.

Tasha and Tanya knew better than to come into the basement when the dope parties started. They had learned the hard way one night when both girls slipped out of bed, traveled down the stairs and peeked though the banister. They had done it so many times that they didn't worry about getting caught until Tasha got her head stuck between the posts and cried out for help.

"That's what you get," Linda said as she wiggled the girl's head loose from the banister. "Now go to bed!"

The close call made Linda think that she had lost control of her house. She needed to think of a better way to make money. If she was going to regain control of her dope parties, she would have to find a reliable drug dealer to supply the house.

She thought about her dilemma as she hung laundry on the clothesline behind her house. She noticed Mr. Mendes, a well-known drug dealer, lean over the fence and wink in her direction. He had a tracheal tube in his throat and spoke in a whisper, and Linda had to concentrate on his every word.

"Hey there, lady. What you doing out here working on a pretty day? You should be partying at Bellevue Square Day."

"Yeah, I know," Linda said. "I ain't got no ride over to that side of town."

"You do now," he said.

Except for his throat condition, Mr. Mendes was a beautiful man. He had a deep Hershey-chocolate complexion that reminded her of Alvin. He dressed in style and had money in his pocket. Linda's heart skipped a beat. She didn't have to think twice about accepting the offer to accompany Mr. Mendes to Bellevue Square Day at the housing project where her grandmother lived.

"What time you want to go?" she said.

"I'll wait. Get ready."

"I got my girls."

"Bring them," he said. "I like kids."

Linda dropped the few sheets she had been holding into the laundry basket. "Wait here," she said.

Mr. Mendes nodded.

Linda rushed inside her apartment. She took a quick shower and fixed herself up in the mirror before she yelled for Tanya to help Tasha get dressed.

"Where we going?" said Tanya, now seven.

"Bellevue Square Day," Linda said.

"For real!" Tanya said.

"Get dressed," Linda yelled louder than she intended. Linda was excited about a chance to go out with a man with a reputation for taking care of all of his women. He was married but that didn't bother Linda because she didn't plan on dating him. This was business, she thought.

Mr. Mendes gave the girls candy during their first outing, and on subsequent dates he brought Linda a pocketful of food stamps, even though she hadn't asked him for anything. He worked a straight job, and made lots of extra cash selling dope that he kept around the city. He used single mothers like Linda to hold his stash. Though he was a drug dealer, Mr. Mendes didn't use drugs and he didn't like his women risking his business by using it. Linda knew all of this, but she didn't see any harm in asking Mr. Mendes to become her supplier.

"I need somebody like you 'round here," Linda said.

"Somebody like me?" he said.

"Yeah, somebody like you," Linda said.

Linda explained that she needed a supplier for her parties. He already knew what she was about, and he agreed to bring her ten bags a day if she used her house to stash the rest of his dope. She could sell five bags for him and sell five bags for herself. Linda agreed to the deal without thinking of the consequences. She promised herself that if Mr. Mendes continued to be good to her, they wouldn't have a problem.

The dope money was good. Linda charged her customers fifteen dollars a bag, plus three dollars each for the needles and another two dollars if they needed to use the narcotics in her basement. Suddenly, Linda was back in control and she was making money hand over fist. Some nights, Linda sold out and had to call Mr. Mendes to restock her supply. Her apartment was the shooting gallery for Vietnam vets and many others who liked a taste on the weekends.

Their arrangement lasted three years. Mr. Mendes made sure that Linda didn't have any problems with the police.

In the spring of 1979, Linda stopped paying attention to her children. She was getting high when Tanya missed twenty six days of school. People in the neighborhood called The Welfare office's confidential telephone line to report that Linda was leaving her children at home by themselves. Her troubles came to a head when Linda overdosed in the bathtub.

Tanya had knocked on the bathroom door for nearly an hour. She got frustrated that Linda wouldn't let her inside.

"I gotta go. I gotta go," Tanya cried as tears streamed down her face. Linda didn't respond, so Tanya pushed away the towels lying on the floor, and went inside to use the toilet.

"Mommy?" Tanya said once she saw Linda's arms hanging off the side of the tub through the shower curtain. "Mommy!"

Linda was in the bathtub unconscious with a needle in her arm. Her eyes had rolled back in her head. Tanya thought she was dead.

"Mommy," Tanya yelled. "What's wrong? Mommy wake up!"

Linda didn't move. Tanya bolted down the stairs and out of the apartment door for help. She didn't think about anything but saving her mother. Tanya knocked on Miss Mary's door wearing panties and a T-shirt. Her appearance frightened the elderly neighbor, who tried unsuccessfully to calm Tanya down. The child was hysterical.

"Mommy dead," Tanya screamed. "She won't wake up."

Miss Mary ushered Tanya into her apartment. "Sit here, baby," Miss Mary told Tanya as she patted the sofa covered in plastic. She covered the child with a bed sheet, then reached for the telephone and called the police, who summoned an ambulance.

Miss Mary had lived next door to Linda for nearly a decade. The walls between their apartments were paper thin, and she wasn't surprised that Linda had taken an overdose. She waited on the sofa trying to comfort Tanya until she heard the sirens. Tanya had fallen asleep when the paramedics and a police officer knocked on her door.

"In there," Miss Mary said, pointing to Linda's apartment. "This child came over here terrified. Her Momma is bad off. Go see about her. Her name is Linda Jordan. She uses them drugs."

Miss Mary kept her eyes fixed outside the window. She prayed silently that Tanya would stay asleep until the drama was over next door. But she also wondered about the whereabouts of Linda's other daughter.

The police and paramedics carried Linda's limp body out of the apartment in a stretcher and placed her inside the ambulance. Once the hospital workers brought Linda back into consciousness, they left her with very few options. She had overdosed with her child in the house. If she didn't go to Cedar Crest, a psychiatric hospital that cared for suicidal drug addicts, the hospital social worker warned that Linda might lose her children.

"Where are my babies now?" Linda asked.

"We don't know," the hospital worker said.

"My babies were asleep in the apartment," Linda said. "Please let me use the telephone. Then I'll go to Cedar Crest. Please let me use the telephone."

Linda called her girlfriend Thelma, who answered the telephone on the second ring. Once Linda explained her dilemma, Thelma, a good friend since Linda moved to the Kings, didn't ask any questions. She agreed to go and see about her children.

"When you coming back?" Thelma asked.

"I don't know," Linda said.

"Don't worry. I got you," Thelma said before hanging up the telephone.

Thelma found Tanya on the floor watching TV at Miss Mary's apartment. She was immediately concerned because Tasha wasn't there.

"What about the other child?" Thelma asked Miss Mary.

"I don't know. I figured she was staying with relatives. I don't know," she said, shaking her head.

Thelma was cool headed. She put Tanya on her hip and went looking for Tasha.

"I want my Mommy," Tanya whined.

"I know, baby, but let's go find your sister first."

"She sleep," Tanya offered.

"Where?"

"In her bed. Mommy beat me when I wake her up," Tanya said.

Tasha proved that day that she could sleep through a storm,

even if it was a man-made one. Thelma collected Linda's girls and changes of clothes for them. She allowed Tanya and Tasha to stay with her until Linda's sister was ready to pick them up or her friend weathered the storm of kicking her addiction, something she hadn't done before.

Linda called home every day, but weeks passed before she was released from the locked ward. She had completed the detoxification part of her treatment, but she was agitated and depressed on the day a hospital social worker found her rifling through an ashtray for a cigarette.

"You need a smoke?" he said.

"Yeah," Linda said.

The social worker concluded that Linda had a healthy personality and a wry sense of humor. She was competent to care for her daughters, if she stayed off heroin. Linda had impressed him until her mood changed. She got angry once he explained that she'd need to stay at the Cedar Crest hospital for another twenty eight days and had to participate in court-ordered group meetings.

"What if I don't?" Linda said.

"The judge will send you to prison," he said. She knew he meant it.

"I'll go," Linda said. "I need to get home. My babies need me."

Two days later, Linda put on the clothes her sister had brought her. She walked out of Cedar Crest vowing that she was finished with using dope and getting locked up at a psychiatric hospital. The male social worker believed her and promised to call her about scheduling a follow-up appointment. Linda looked refreshed when he showed up at her apartment about a month later. She had gained weight. She told him she had stopped using heroin. It was a lie.

"I ain't going back down that crooked road no more," Linda told him. She poured a cup of tea for the worker. "I go to the group meetings when I can. I would go more often, but it's hard without a bus pass and a babysitter."

The social worker left impressed. He wrote in his progress report that Linda had been kind and cooperative, but he was concerned that her husband, who was also an addict, had come home from prison. The feds dropped the case against him after he pleaded guilty in Hartford. It had all been a bluff. Alvin refused to come downstairs to speak to the social worker when she called him. When the social worker tried to check up on her again, Linda's telephone number had been changed to an unpublished number. She hadn't responded to his letters, and other cases overwhelmed him. He placed Linda's case in his closed case file cabinet.

Other social workers at Kinsella Elementary School were accustomed to dealing with difficult parents like Linda, who didn't want to be bothered with their concerns and questions. They were repeatedly knocking on Linda's door to talk to her about Tanya. The second-grader was chronically absent, and had told her teacher that her mother had punched her in the mouth. Though the teacher didn't see any marks on Tanya, she called The Welfare office to report her complaint as a case of potential child abuse. The school called Linda for a meeting. She was always uncomfortable about going to mandatory conferences with Tanya's teachers and the social worker. She showed her discontent when she answered their probing questions.

"We called you here today because we are concerned about Tanya," the teacher said. "She is not coming to school regularly and she has reported ..."

"That child is driving me crazy." Linda interrupted. "She is a born liar, and yes, I beat her ass sometimes."

The professionals in the room froze. They noticed that Linda was holding her younger daughter Tasha a little too tightly throughout most of the conference. They also saw that the toddler had a serious rash on her scalp, something that looked like it needed a doctor's attention.

"She's been sick," Linda volunteered when she noticed the workers staring at Tasha. "She is getting better. I took her to the clinic and they gave her some medicine."

Tasha fidgeted. Linda grew impatient and directed the conversation to the bottom line. "Tanya is jealous of her baby sister," Linda said. "She is disrespectful to her father who can't stay out of prison long enough for her to get to know him."

"Who does she like?" the social worker asked.

"Daddy Harry, she loves him better than the rest of us," said Linda. She agreed to go to counseling with her oldest daughter if it would help.

"Do you think that will stop her from screaming and waking up the neighbors at night?" the social worker asked.

"I sure hope so," Linda said.

The social workers who rallied on Tanya's behalf concluded

that Linda was using Tanya as a scapegoat for many of her troubles. "If you hit her again, the police will be called," one worker said.

Linda's case was reopened before the ink was dry on their agreement. An anonymous tipper called police to report that Linda had left the children alone in the house. The desk sergeant who pulled Linda's address from the case files, and saw Alvin's criminal rap sheet, was immediately convinced that both parents weren't at fault. Alvin answered the door when the cops showed up to check on the children. He told them that Linda walked out the front door during an argument and he had walked out of the back door. When he returned to the house hours later, the children were sitting on the floor all alone. He said he fed them and they were asleep.

"Keep it up and you and your wife will be in lockup," the sergeant warned.

"Why ya'll bothering me? I'm here. I'm did what I was supposed to do," Alvin said.

"Keep it up," the sergeant said.

Alvin and Linda's marital troubles progressed to the point that the police and the social workers were regulars at the Jordan home. Before Memorial Day, Tanya left a message at The Welfare office that her mother was badly beaten by her father. When the worker followed up, Linda said that she and Alvin had been arguing all week. She told him to leave and he hit her, blackening her eye, and kicked her in the stomach. Linda was so upset when the policeman showed up at her door that he threatened to take her to jail. He lost his temper, cuffed her and made her sit on the porch until she calmed down.

"I'm tired of the cops taking sides," Linda sulked later during a conversation with her social worker.

"Are you feeling okay now?"

"They say my kidney is infected," Linda said. "I got to go back to the doctor for me, and for Tasha who still got that rash."

"Tell me how this all came about," the worker said, referring to the fight with Alvin.

"Turns out it was all Tanya's fault. She stole ten dollars in food stamps. When Alvin asked me for money, I went to my secret hiding place and the stamps were gone. He blamed me. That child almost got me killed. I want her out. Can't you send her someplace for the summer? I hear the Times Farms Camp can take her. Help me with that. My Daddy say that he'll pay for Tanya's application fee. He love Tanya about as much as she love him."

Linda also had just about enough of Alvin's antics. He wasn't bringing any money into the house but he was always asking for the money and dope that she kept for Mr. Mendes. She hadn't slept with Mr. Mendes and was careful about what she said to him in front of the girls. But Alvin repeatedly accused her of sleeping around with Mr. Mendes.

"We just friends," Linda said during their last argument.

"Yeah, right. A friend don't buy another man's groceries. And if he do, that woman don't accept them," Alvin said.

"You know damn well why I got him around. He taking care of me and you too. Deal with it," Linda said during one argument.

Alvin knew what Linda said was true. Her friend supplied both of them with money and dope. He was also making an impression on his daughters who called him everything but Daddy. Mr. Mendes was bringing more to the table than he was, and Alvin didn't like it.

Alvin slept with the girl next door when she gave him some time and attention. He knew Linda would find out, but he didn't care. He knew that Mr. Mendes wasn't a pushover like Countryman. Alvin felt he had to get back at Linda in the only way he could.

Linda reached her breaking point when she heard about the affair. Her body was tired from the dope but her mind stayed focused on the best way to hurt Alvin. She got of bed and went to the closet they shared. Her money had paid for his suits, his wingtip shoes, his shirts and the applejack-style hats he sported when he went out with other women. She wondered what he would do without his stuff.

She ripped his wardrobe from the hangers and dropped every suit, shirt and pair of jeans in a pile on the floor. She stomped his shoes until they were out of shape and his fine lines were wrinkled. But that wasn't enough. Linda opened the bedroom window and threw each piece outside into the pouring rain. His clothes were drenched when Alvin finally banged on the front door that Linda had locked with double-bolts. Alvin was high and he didn't immediately notice that he was walking over his tailor-made suits and silk shirts littered on the ground amongst the empty bottles and trash. He bent down and picked up one of his shirts.

"What the hell?" he yelled. "Linda! Get out here."

Linda heard Alvin making a fuss outside. She stayed in her bed and pulled the covers over her head. She didn't feel like being bothered. He had betrayed her with the girl next door, and nothing he said now would make her open her door.

"How the hell you goin' put me out?" Alvin screamed. "You hiding that nigga in there. If you is, I'm goin' kick your ass."

He knocked and kicked at the door until he became defeated. He knew if he kept it up, the lady next door would call the police, so he knocked on another door until it opened.

CHAPTER 13 | MR. MENDES

ALVIN'S BETRAYAL PUSHED LINDA DEEPER into her depression. She drank liquor and used heroin when she had it. She hardly left her bedroom and when she did, she was rarely sober enough to navigate the stairs without falling. Her body reeked of cigarettes. She kept boxes of dry sugar-coated cereal on her dresser and stored cans of sodas in a miniature refrigerator that she kept locked because that's where she also stored her needles and dope.

Linda packed up her girls after the explosion with Alvin and sent them to live with her family for their summer vacation. Their absence made it easy for her to stay in her bed for weeks until her supply of dope dried up. The malaise she felt lifted once she took a bath. The warm water she poured over her head gave her a new clarity. She looked around and saw the condition of her apartment. Dirty clothes were piled all over the place. The floors were caked with dirt and the dishes in the kitchen sink smelled of food marinating in sour dishwater. The sight of her apartment made Linda mull over what she loved about Alvin. He was the kind of addict who got energized when he used heroin. He cleaned when he was home and he never went to bed without making sure the house was spic and span. Alvin would curse out Linda if he came home and saw the deplorable condition of the apartment.

She shrugged off her daydream and grabbed the broom, sweeping the trash into big piles in the middle of each room. She was tired, but motivated. She got on her knees in the bathroom and rubbed away the rings of nasty film and caked dirt around the tub, the face bowl and the toilet bowl. Sweat dripped from her forehead when she headed into her bedroom, where she pulled the nasty sheets off the bed and placed them in a washtub that she filled with hot water, laundry detergent and bleach.

Hours passed before she was finished cleaning. Her hair and nightgown were wet with sweat. She showered for a second time, dressed in a pair of jeans that sagged around her behind and a dress shirt that showed off her petite frame. Her work wasn't done. She rinsed her laundry and took the basket out to the clothesline. She thought about Alvin as she angrily shook out the sheets.

"Two could play that game," Linda said to herself.

She decided at that moment that it was time for her to get even. She would give Mr. Mendes a shot if he gave her the opportunity. They hadn't done anything romantic since Mr. Mendes was supplying her with dope, but Linda knew he was interested in getting her between the sheets. She thought about ways to seduce him as she pulled her clothes off of the clothesline. Her resolve grew once she saw Alvin coming out of her neighbor's back door. He was driving the woman's car and brazen about their affair. Everyone in the neighborhood was talking about how Alvin had done Linda wrong.

"He ain't trying to hide what he doing," Linda told Thelma, who showed up unannounced one day.

"Time for you to move on," Thelma said. "That man is giving you the blues and bringing you down. Just look at you, Linda! When is the last time you did something nice for yourself and your girls? Where are they? I ain't seen them since Alvin moved in with that girl."

The journey Linda had traveled since the night she threw Alvin out made her sad. She cried, something she hadn't done since her binge.

"I'm trying," Linda lied. "It's hard when he doing it right here in front my face. If I catch that bitch by herself, I got something for her."

"Don't go there," Thelma said. "She might be at fault but he using her to get to you. You know why Alvin picked that girl. He don't really want to be over there. He's fooling with her, because he know he ain't no match for Mendes."

Linda perked up when she heard Mr. Mendes' name. She hadn't seen him since she kicked the junkies out of her apartment. She missed him, his dope and his money. She didn't like the fact that Mr. Mendes was married and dedicated to his wife. Getting him in her bed would be difficult. Linda knew she would never have him for herself.

"I'm thinking about gettin' with him," Linda told Thelma.

"Getting with him," Thelma said.

"Gettin' with him," Linda laughed.

"Be careful. A married man ain't nothing to play with. You

play with fire," Thelma said. "You know the rest."

Linda spent the rest of the afternoon catching up on her stories and thinking about her decision. "Fuck it," Linda told herself. She was out of dope.

When Mr. Mendes showed up at the door, Linda was wearing a red nightgown. He made it clear that their agreement to store his dope hadn't changed. He was all too willing to give her the romance she desired. The sex between them was hot and steamy, but Linda missed the passion she had with Alvin. After the first few times, Linda felt empty when Mr. Mendes got up and put on his clothes before the sun went down. Thelma's warning had become a reality. Linda wasn't comfortable with sharing a man with his wife, but she was satisfied when she knew that Alvin would eventually cross paths with Mr. Mendes outside her door.

Linda's trap backfired on the evening when she let Mr. Mendes out of the back door. Alvin was sitting outside on the stoop. She saw the hurt in Alvin's eyes and it made her feel as guilty as she did years before when he caught her using dope. She thought she would be gratified once she paid Alvin back, but the guilt she felt about her own infidelity was overwhelming.

She retired to her bedroom until the day her children came home. She told her sister to drop off her girls at the back door and she waited for them there, hoping that Alvin wouldn't knock on her door. Alvin was waiting in the shadows and he walked up to greet the girls when they exited the car carrying sleeping bags and a basket of dirty laundry.

"Daddy," Tanya yelled. "Daddy."

Tasha thought of Mr. Mendes as her father figure. But Tanya knew her daddy, though she didn't like the way he treated her mother. When they fought, Tanya took on the same sort of responsibilities around the house that Linda had as a child. Alvin got on Linda's nerves and caused a lot of unnecessary drama for her family. Once Linda heard Tanya yelling for Daddy, she knew Alvin would manipulate the situation into a reunion.

"Damn," she cursed. "Com' on." She ushered the girls inside the screen door and slammed it shut in Alvin's face.

"Bye, Daddy," Tanya waved.

"Bye, baby girl," Alvin winked.

"Hey, Linda," he said before Linda closed the outer door.

"That motherfucker thinks he's slick," Linda said.

"I want to see my Daddy," Tanya said.

"Not now!" Linda said, louder than she wanted. "Not now."

Linda was cooking eggs for the girls when Alvin showed up the following day. He demanded to see his daughters, but Linda wasn't ready.

"Linda, Linda," Alvin said as he knocked on the window in the kitchen.

Linda shut the window, closed the curtains and turned up the radio. "Tanya! Tasha! Come get these eggs," Linda yelled as she walked out of the kitchen and left the girls' plates on the table.

When Alvin stepped in Linda's path later that day, she wasn't surprised and she kept walking. She knew exactly why Alvin was pushing up against her. It was check day and Linda was on her way to the mailbox to pick up her monthly check and her food stamps. She pretended that she hadn't heard Alvin whispering in her ear and she picked up her pace.

"That's how you want it now?" Alvin said. "All right, then."

Linda diverted her eyes upward into the autumn-colored trees and away from Alvin's deep penetrating gaze. It took all her strength now not to look at him and she held in her breath as so not to smell his sweet cologne. She felt ten years old again, playing hard to get with Alvin, an irresistible boy from the 'hood.

Linda knew that Alvin would always be somebody who wanted what he wanted when he wanted it. He kept showing up at her door with a full heart, sweet cocoa lips and large empty hands. His presence had Linda wondering whether he would be different this time. She found herself dressing better and fixing her hair when she went outside for small things. Linda knew how to fish and she knew how to flirt. She decided to reel Alvin in for the long haul.

Alvin had spent much of his adult life around prison guards, and he was as demanding as they could be when he had the upper hand. But he hadn't raised his voice once during his maddening dance with Linda. He wanted to knock her silly when she refused to allow him inside her apartment to see the girls. He kept his cool for weeks.

He had set a trap for all his girls. Candy for the little ones and kindness for Linda, a woman he had loved since they were kids. He offered to help out with the girls when Linda worked nights cleaning office buildings. She didn't like the fact that Alvin wouldn't look for work, but if he were serious about watching the girls, it would make things easier for both of them. Linda knew that once she finished her day work, she wouldn't have to worry about cleaning her own house if she left Alvin a little something in the kitchen drawer. He would cook, clean and put the girls to bed. Prison had ingrained that kind of discipline in a man who couldn't seem to find his way in the world.

It took weeks before she let Alvin spend an entire night. She shared the dope that she stored for Mr. Mendes with Alvin, but she liked how he did things around the house when dope was flowing through his veins. She hadn't forgotten about Alvin's fling, but she was willing to forget if he begged her for forgiveness. Alvin wasn't good at begging. He had never been a humble man, so Linda knew he meant business when he said the words she had been waiting to hear.

"What a man gotta do to get his family back?"

The stalemate between Linda and Alvin didn't last long and their relationship went sour after Linda had two consecutive miscarriages. She drank heavily after the loss of each baby she called her lost boys, and she was a mean and angry drunk. She kept a bottle of rum by her bedside and she pitched a fit anytime anyone asked her to slow down. She was drinking so much that Mr. Mendes backed into the shadows when she messed up one of the packages and didn't have the money to cover the dope. He cared about Linda, but he didn't trust her to continue to keep his dope while sharing the narcotics that she promised to sell with Alvin.

Linda was cranky and uptight once Mr. Mendes cut her off and stopped coming around. She used her sharp tongue when she didn't have dope. She fought with Alvin, who didn't try to

look for work. Their relationship turned increasingly more vola-
tile and Tanya became adept at calling 911 when her parents
started fighting. The police operators had also become so accustomed to hearing the child's voice that they were nonchalant
about her calls. When the police didn't show up immediately,
Tanya pulled Tasha under the bottom bunk bed and covered
their heads with blankets. The two of them would be under the
bed when the police officer arrived to charge Linda and Alvin
for disorderly conduct. Linda didn't have a criminal record so
she wasn't carted off to jail, but Alvin generally went to jail in
the back of a cruiser and was held overnight if Linda didn't have
the money to bail him out. The maddening dance between the
couple was both explosive and passionate.

Before Linda knew it, she was pregnant and meeting with
her social worker about her troubles at home. Her file was listed
as an active abuse case, but her new worker was naïve and didn't
press for more counseling after Linda went to the court and
obtained a restraining order against Alvin. "I'm divorcing him,"
Linda told her worker during a home visit in July 1978.

The previous night, Linda and Alvin had exchanged punch-
es, leaving both with black eyes and fat lips. The police took
them both to jail. One night in jail precipitated Linda's resolve
that Alvin wasn't worth all that drama.

The social worker, who was new to her job, didn't know the
signs of a classic abuse case and was easily manipulated by both
Linda and Alvin. When she talked to Linda, the worker believed
that Alvin was the villain, a chronic drug addict who beat up his
wife when she refused him money for drugs. But she got con-

fused when Alvin complained that Linda never cooked, drank all the time, and was always leaving their children in the house alone. In another interview with Linda, the worker noticed that she was intoxicated. She was angry and defensive when the worker told her what Alvin had said about her.

"Damn liar," Linda screamed. "You gonna believe him over me?"

"Calm down, Mrs. Jordan," the worker said.

"You calm down," Linda retorted before she left the room and slammed the door.

The following day, Linda showed up at Tanya's school to address what school officials had labeled chronic absenteeism. Linda smelled of alcohol. The secretary at the front desk took note of this and passed it to the teachers who would discuss Tanya's fate.

"I'm here to see Tanya's teachers," Linda slurred.

"Tanya?" said the secretary, who kept track of all of the parent-teacher appointments.

"Tanya Jordan. I mean Tanya Shannon," Linda said.

"Let me call the social worker," the secretary said.

"The social worker? This is some bullshit. I'm outta here," Linda said.

"Wait! I found the conference date on my list," the secretary said. "Wait! Take a seat over there."

Linda sat on the wooden bench until the teacher showed up in the office. The teacher, who had a kind and cherubic face, spoke in a whisper around parents who didn't want to be there. Her smile was infectious.

"Mrs. Jordan," the teacher said as she tapped Linda on the shoulder. "Mrs. Jordan?"

Linda had nodded off. She had gotten high before she got dressed for her appointment. Some of the buttons on her blouse were unbuttoned, and her attire was too small for her bulging belly. Linda heard the teacher at her side but it took a moment for her to get her bearings.

"Sorry, sorry," she slurred. "Was I 'posed to come here today?" Linda asked as she wiped the sleep from her eyes. "I can't keep my times straight. This baby is kicking my butt."

"Baby?" the teacher asked.

"Yeah, I'm expectin.' I can't believe that Alvin is putting me through this again. Seems like every time I look around my ass is having another one of his babies," Linda said as the teacher escorted her down the hallway to the teacher-conference room. The concrete floor hurt Linda's feet. She didn't have on the right shoes and her demeanor turned sour once she saw the school's social worker sitting in the conference room.

"Have you been to the doctor?" the teacher asked.

"Not yet," Linda said.

The school's worker hadn't done a thorough review of Linda's history. She listened in sympathy as Linda embellished her life story. But she couldn't help thinking that Linda, a high school dropout, didn't value education for her daughter.

Tanya had missed two and a half years of school and rarely attended a full week. The social worker had concluded, before Linda entered the conference room, that Tanya's problems in school were due principally to the problems she faced at home.

Linda, the worker reported, was angry, hostile and upset that she had not been a better parent. Her conclusions hinged on Tanya's statements that her mother partied into the night and was asleep when she was supposed to prepare her oldest daughter for school.

"Maybe counseling might help," the social worker recommended.

"Counseling? Why did you think I need counseling?" Linda said sarcastically.

"Maybe it would help Tanya?" she said.

Linda didn't like the tone of the conversation. She had a hangover and had no intentions of taking her girls to counseling, but she signed off on Tanya's educational plan because she knew it would get the teachers and the school's social worker off her back.

Linda mumbled to herself as she walked back down the corridor of Tanya's school. "I need a damn drink," she said.

"Say what?" the teacher said.

"Oh, nothing," Linda said. "I need to think."

CHAPTER 14 | FOOTSTEPS

NICOLE WAS BORN IN THE WINTER OF 1978. She was a Christmas present during tough times. Linda's income from The Welfare had never been sufficient, and she hoped that after the baby was born Alvin would find a legitimate job.

He didn't. He liked his lifestyle of gambling, using dope and stealing anything that wasn't nailed down. Once Linda reconciled to herself that Alvin was on his way back to prison, their relationship ventured back down a rocky road. When Alvin wasn't getting high, he was fighting with Linda over money and little things that should not have mattered.

Nicole became Tanya's responsibility when she wasn't in school. She'd feed her a bottle, warm cereal and juice for the next four years. She liked taking care of her baby sister more than Tasha because she was too young to argue and she slept soundly on the nights that Tanya, now past puberty, invited boys into their bedroom. She liked boys and hanging out with her cousins when her parents were too high to care.

Tanya's secret love affair revealed itself after she missed a few periods and Linda noticed that her fifteen-year-old daughter was in the family way. She was following the same track as her mother. Linda had been a teenage mother, and she noticed the signs that Tanya might be pregnant when she once asked for a second piece of chicken. She had never been a big eater.

"Getting pregnant is easy," Linda told her one night while Tanya was washing dishes. "Taking care of a baby is another thing. You ain't having this baby."

Tanya nodded in agreement. But Linda promised her daughter that taking care of her problem would not be traumatic. She didn't want Tanya's abortion to be a black mark in the same way that Linda's had been when she got pregnant at 13. She explained the medical procedure before they got to the back alley clinic, so Tanya wasn't frightened when it was time to place her bare feet into the icy cold stirrups.

"This will stay between us," Linda said. "You need to start keeping your mouth and your legs shut. "You understand?"

"Yes, mama," answered Tanya, relieved that Linda hasn't asked any questions about the boy she had sex with.

Tanya paid close attention to her younger sisters and kept them out of Linda's hair as payment for her mother's secrecy. She was still interested in boys, but she was cautious for the next few years. She promised Linda that she would wake her in time to take her to school so the social workers would also stay off her back. That promise lasted until Linda and Alvin began fighting again. Tanya was thankful when Alvin left the apartment without being forced to leave by the police. She saw that Linda was trying to become a better parent despite her troubles with Alvin.

Tanya's pregnancy gave Linda flashbacks about her own troubled childhood. She begged Alvin to help her out around the house when he came back around, but he refused to do something for nothing. One night, Linda made dinner as a peace offering. There was no dope in the house and he was anxious and jumpy. Linda pulled his shirttail and Alvin popped her in the mouth. Before Tanya knew it, her parents were tussling on the kitchen floor. She jumped in and Tasha was right behind her. They were wrestling on the floor when Tanya started screaming.

"Stop it! Stop it!" she yelled as she lunged at her mother, who had the upper hand. "The police coming! You watch."

Linda took her foot off of Alvin's neck. He ran for the door and slammed it behind him. Linda flew into a rage at her children.

"You gonna take his side. *His* side!" Linda yelled. She sunk her teeth into Tanya's tiny left breast until Tanya yelled for help.

Linda was already mad at Tanya for allowing Tasha and Nicole to play with matches. They set a mattress on fire, but she hadn't confronted them because they put it out quickly. Linda didn't want the police and social workers to force her into another meeting. Now, her two oldest girls whom she had cared for most of their lives, had taken Alvin's side that night on the kitchen floor, and their betrayal was unforgivable.

The disturbance woke Linda's neighbors who called the police. Linda was throwing both girls out the house when they arrived. Tanya was okay with leaving, but seven-year-old Tasha fought back. Linda was choking Tasha on the front porch when Officer Massicotte rushed to assist the child. He pushed Linda away from Tasha, handcuffed her and forced her into the back of a squad car that arrived as backup. Tanya, Tasha and baby Nicole were hiding under a bed when the officer walked into the house to get them.

"I won't hurt you," the policeman said. "Come on, girls. I won't hurt you."

He sounded sincere. Tanya crawled out first. She looked at the officer and searched his face.

"Come on, y'all," she said. "Can you take us to my aunt's house?"

"Get your stuff," the officer said.

Massicotte heard Linda screaming outside and he rushed to get the girls to safety.

"Get that one out of my sight. I don't care where you take that bitch!" Linda pointed at Tasha.

Massicotte told Tanya that he could take the girls to see their auntie. "You ever been in a police car? Buckle up."

"Yeah," Tanya said once the girls settled in the back seat.

"I can't believe Linda bit me," she said.

Massicotte hadn't thought to check for bruises. He stopped the car and turned to face the girls, who were talking to each other. He overheard that Linda had bitten Tanya on the breast. Tasha said her mother had beaten her up in the bathtub. Nicole was too afraid to speak.

"She hits you?" Massicotte probed.

"Yep," Tanya said, pointing to her tiny chest. "She bit me right here."

"And she ... and she, choked and pushed me in the bathtub," Tasha volunteered.

Tanya pinched Tasha in the arm.

"Awl," Tasha screamed. She immediately regretted snitching on her mother.

"No more of that, young lady," the officer said. "You want me to take you to jail?"

"Noo," Tanya said firmly. "Is my mommy coming back? She didn't hurt us that bad. She was just mad at us right now."

Massicotte didn't consult the girls when he took a U-turn toward St. Francis Hospital that evening in 1982. It was his duty to ensure the Jordan girls weren't injured before he put them into somebody else's care.

"Where we going?" Tanya asked. "This ain't the way."

"I know. I'm going to get all of you checked out at the hospital first."

"Hospital?" Tanya gasped. "We okay. I promise. Just take us to see Auntie. Linda didn't hurt us that bad."

Massicotte was not a rookie. He had been on the police force long enough to recognize the signs of classic child abuse. Tanya was convincing, but he didn't want to be blamed if the girls had injuries that he couldn't immediately see.

"It won't take long," he promised.

Tanya removed her hand from the back of the officer's shoulder and sat back. She was mad at her mother, but she never intended to get her in trouble. She didn't like the way this was going but she didn't know how to change the course of what Tasha had said.

Just as Tanya had suspected, the hospital staff summoned a social worker to the examining room. The woman peppered her with questions.

"Did your mother do this to you?"

"No, I fell," Tanya lied.

"That's not true," the worker said. "Did your mother do this to you?"

"It don't hurt that bad," Tanya said of the bite wound.

After the nurses bandaged the wound and gave her a shot in her butt, Tanya watched as they stripped Tasha down to her underwear.

"No," Tasha said, following her older sister's lead.

The nurses didn't find any wounds on Tasha's body and they told her to get dressed. The girls were told to sit quietly until the police officer returned to take them to see their aunt. The older girls kept quiet, afraid that anything they said would be used to hurt Linda.

The city jail was worse than anything Linda imagined. Linda balled her body in a corner of the holding cell and covered her nose to block out the smell. She stayed like that until a female officer opened the bars and beckoned for her to follow her into a van en route to Niantic, the state's prison for women, where she would spend the night. Linda feared prison worse than gambling with death each time she stuck a needle in her arm.

"Tomorrow you will see a judge," said the heavyset white cop. "This your first time?"

Linda nodded.

A heroin jones was crashing down on her shoulders and she found it hard to stand up. She needed a fix and had no way to stop her stomach cramps and the chills from inching up her arms. She couldn't escape the smell inside the van that other prisoners left behind. The ride was miserable and it showed on her face.

"You all right?" the guard asked once they made it inside the institution.

Linda didn't answer.

"You don't have to say anything. A fool could see you need a fix."

Linda was unfamiliar with these types of surroundings. She focused her attention on the gray concrete walls inside the prison's holding cell to avoid eye contact with the other prisoners. She felt cold throughout the night and the thin gray blanket was not enough to warm her. Linda felt relieved when a guard called her name. She was ushered back into the van, which had heat, and she relaxed during another two-hour ride back to Hartford.

It was still dark outside when she got back to the holding cell in the courthouse basement. The wait there was long. She guessed at the time of day when the guard gave her a bologna sandwich but she wasn't sure whether the sandwich was meant to be breakfast or lunch. She couldn't bring herself to eat it. She ignored her stomach pains because she was worried about the whereabouts of her daughters. She knew she looked scared, but gathered herself and regained her composure when her name was finally called.

She went to court enough times with Alvin to know if she went into the courtroom with an attitude the outcome of her criminal case would be detrimental. She forced a look of contrition when Dennis O'Connor, the male prosecutor, asked her about the events of the previous night.

"I was high and drunk," Linda said. "I lost control."

O'Connor hadn't expected such candor. He knew that Linda hadn't been arrested before and a report from the hospital revealed that her girls weren't seriously injured. He agreed with the police sergeant not to press charges if Linda didn't resist going to John Dempsey Hospital for treatment. Linda didn't know the hand she had been dealt behind her back. She was afraid when the judge called her name a second time.

"Your honor, we've come to an agreement," said O'Connor, who spoke directly to the judge after a recess. Linda wasn't asked to respond and she didn't know what was going on. "Mrs. Jordan admits that she was out of control last night. She wants to go into treatment for the next 28 days. The state is willing to drop the charges if she successfully completes the program."

"Drop the charges," Linda mouthed to herself. "Now, that's what I'm talking about."

"Excuse me, Mrs. Jordan. Do you have something to say?" the judge interrupted.

"I messed up," she said.

"If you do what they tell you to do at John Dempsey, you won't need to come here again. Do you understand?"

"Yes, your honor," Linda said as her defense attorney whispered the agreement details into her ear.

She didn't quite understand everything being discussed behind the scenes. After the judge announced the agreement, he nodded with approval when the judicial marshals approached to remove the handcuffs.

"The hospital can't take her until tomorrow," the prosecutor interjected.

A burly white court marshal who was twice Linda's size put the handcuffs back on as she doubled over in pain. He led her back to the van that drove her back to Niantic women's prison for another nine days. Prison wasn't the place for her. It was Alvin's thing. She didn't like being locked up, being told when to eat and sleep. The cold damp building felt a lot like the basement of the tenement where Linda and Vee once practiced using dope for the first time.

Linda slept on a bare mattress with one eye open so she could watch out for the inmates, who circled her bunk hoping to take advantage of the new kid on the block. Her inmate number gave away her status as a new prisoner. The higher the number sown into an inmate's uniform, the lower that inmate ranked on the cellblock.

Linda had heard enough stories. She knew better than to accept offers for combs, brushes, toothbrushes and bars of soap from the inmates. They nicknamed her "Hershey" after the candy bar on the first day she walked the stroll from the dormitory to the mess hall. Though she stayed on guard, Linda couldn't shake off the chill that made it difficult for her not to ask Bertha and the other jailbirds circling her bunk where she could get something to take off the edge. She ignored those inmates who devoured her petite chocolate body with their eyes. When they persisted, Linda went into her crazy act and kicked the metal bars around the bunk bed long enough to get on a lot of people's nerves.

"Just leave her alone," an inmate yelled from the opposite side of the dormitory. "That damn kicking is getting on my damn nerves."

Linda stopped kicking when the jailbirds found other prey. She acknowledged women she recognized from her neighborhood but kept to herself. She was terrified both day and night and that feeling kept her company when she wasn't fighting off her drug withdrawal in the prison infirmary. Linda stared at the concrete walls, ate very little and showered with her clothes on until a guard woke her one morning at three and took her to John Dempsey Hospital. She was released from prison before her family's money orders for the commissary arrived.

John Dempsey Hospital had a drug treatment center. It wasn't home, but at least Linda could order the food she liked. There were no bars covering her window, but Linda had to deal with an internal prison called anger locked in addiction. Every little thing set her off, but she was especially ticked when she found out that Tanya and Tasha, her two oldest daughters, had provided the ammunition the police needed to force her into treatment. She called her sister every day to check on baby Nicole, but when the subject of her other girls came up, she "accidentally on purpose" hung up the telephone. She was mad at them but even madder at Alvin.

The trouble in their relationship was at the root of Linda's problems with drugs and alcohol and she knew it. Rather than deal with the issues she had with him in counseling, Linda cut Alvin off when she signed the divorce papers from her hospital bed. She sent them to him in prison in the fall of 1982. Dis-

solving her marriage seemed like the right thing to do after the
state Department of Children and Families forced Linda and her
girls into counseling. Linda knew the court officials would look
favorably on her decision. She was tired of fighting with Alvin
and explaining to cops and social workers why she kept taking
Alvin back into the home when they had such a dysfunctional
relationship. Linda got scared when a new social worker recommended that her girls live temporarily with her aunt and older
sister. It wasn't that she didn't need the break, but she feared
losing her housing subsidy without having a good paying job.
Linda knew she could lose the girls to strangers if she forced the
issue against the temporary placement, and her girls would be
shipped away into the state's massive foster care system.

She knew what foster care was like. For a brief time, when
she was twelve years old, Linda was forced into a foster home
after she swallowed a bottle of aspirin. She didn't stay there long,
but she knew what abandonment felt like and she didn't want
that for her daughters. She hated the thought of her girls living
with people who got paid by the state to take care of them.

Linda packed up her girls as soon as she was released from
the hospital. They were ready to go before the social workers had
time to draw up the papers. She gave her older sister fifty dollars
in cash and fifty dollars in food stamps when she visited her in
the hospital so it would look like she had been a responsible
parent. She didn't like Tanya staying with her younger sister, because her sister didn't enforce a curfew, but if Tanya wanted to
run wild, Linda thought, she was old enough to learn about the
lessons of the streets. She asked the social worker if her two

youngest girls could go to live with her Aunt Rosie, who had a three-bedroom apartment, kept a clean house and didn't have junkies running in and out. That arrangement seemed to work out until Linda heard that one of her aunt's friends had touched Nicole in an inappropriate way.

Linda stepped up her counseling sessions and secretly substituted her heroin habit with pints of rum and vodka to take the edge off. She was stumbling in the footsteps of her mother when Tasha and Nicole were allowed to come home.

CHAPTER 15 | POSITIVE

LINDA WAS DOWNTOWN ONE DAY when she ran into Alvin's cousin Logan at the bus stop. Logan was a distant cousin who she didn't see much but always liked. She noticed that he was in bad shape. He looked haggard and was walking with a cane.

"Hey, where you trying to go?"

"Oh, hey Linda, I came down here to check out Male Image. I need to buy a suit," he said.

Linda took him by the arm and they started to walk.

"Let's go," she said.

Linda couldn't help but wonder what had happened to Logan. He didn't look good. The wrinkled clothes were out of character for Logan, who normally wore the latest fashions and traveled with a bunch of his friends when he went shopping. But that day, he was alone. He looked like he needed a friend.

"You still picking up?" Linda asked.

"Yeah," Logan said. "What about you?"

"Nah, I'm trying to kick that habit," Linda said. "It's dragging me down."

"How is Alvin?

"Same," Linda responded.

Logan just smiled like he always did. He didn't say I told you so, something that Linda knew he was thinking as they walked toward the men's store. Logan wasn't the type to rub it in.

When they made it to the store, he walked toward the back to the clearance rack where the funeral black suits were hanging on display. He said he wanted a nice suit for Father's Day. Linda wondered why Logan had decided on a black suit in the summertime when all the colors of the rainbow were on display. But it wasn't her business and she didn't ask. She stayed by Logan, cupping his arm as they walked back to the bus stop with the suit. They promised to keep in touch, something they rarely did.

Linda was surprised the following day when she heard that Logan was in the hospital. Her curiosity made her go to see him, and his sudden decline scared Linda. Rather than judge him or his medical condition, she offered to visit him at the convalescent home once he was released from the hospital. Linda noticed that Logan hadn't had many visitors. He told her that he had AIDS, a new disease, and his friends gradually turned their backs on him.

Linda didn't know much about AIDS, but it aggravated her that Logan's friends had abandoned him and that the staff at the hospital treated Logan "like he was the disease."

Linda didn't like the way the staff made her feel. She didn't like the masks they wore when they entered his room. She hated it when the nurses scolded her for taking off her mask when she sat by Logan's bedside to watch her stories on the TV. She didn't know what the words "infectious disease" meant. But it didn't matter to Linda. Logan was family. She took it upon herself to become his caretaker once he was released and sent to the Hartford Hotel. She didn't like it there.

"That place is nasty," she told Mr. Mendes when she asked him for his car so she could go to see about Alvin's cousin.

Logan was staying in a tiny room abandoned by the rest of the world. He had used the bathroom on himself when Linda went for a visit. There was no one there to help him clean up the mess, so Linda held her nose and did it. Making it to the bathroom was becoming difficult for Logan, who was now using a walker. His condition convinced Linda to take Logan home to live with her family once his disability check from Social Security arrived.

"You can take my bed," she told him. "At my house, you can take a nice bath. Me and my girls goin' to take care of you."

Logan, who had a soft spot in his heart for Linda, was always glad to see her. He didn't say much, but his gratitude showed in his eyes. He was relieved that someone in his family was stepping up to help take care of him. They never discussed his medical condition or how and why he had AIDS.

Logan slept peacefully in Linda's bed for three days while she drank herself to sleep on the couch. He would have stayed in her room longer but his Social Security check arrived. A hospital bed was delivered and Linda set up a room for Logan in her basement.

"What I loved about him was he wasn't afraid of dying," Linda said later. "We joked about it."

"When you die, send me back a number," Linda quipped.

"Oh yeah, Boo. I'll do that," Logan said.

"Do me one more favor?" he asked. "Take my check and spend it on you and your kids. You bet' not take any of that money to bury me."

Linda cashed Logan's check the following day. She brought him flowers. The money Logan contributed to Linda's household didn't cover what she had lost after the regular card parties shut down. But it helped.

Before Logan got sick, Linda had ignored the stories about AIDS on TV about how gay men in San Francisco and New York were dying rapidly of the disease. The newscasters said the medical community had associated unusual kinds of cancers and incurable bouts of pneumonia as symptoms of the disease. It didn't seem real to Linda until somebody in her family was diagnosed. But Linda didn't get nervous until she saw a news report that said AIDS was contagious and that intravenous drug users were spreading the virus with dirty needles and unprotected sex. She started preparing food for Logan on paper plates as a precaution and stopped allowing Tanya to come over to watch the younger girls. Her oldest daughter, who had just turned 16, was pregnant for a second time.

Linda dismissed the signs of her own morning sickness. She wasn't happy about having another one of Alvin's babies in the same way she was when she was pregnant with Tanya. She was concerned because she wasn't ready for another baby. She also knew that Tanya wasn't ready for a baby, either.

Linda didn't tell anyone she was pregnant with her fourth daughter until she started to show. A nurse who visited Logan recommended that Linda and her family get tested for HIV, but she ignored the suggestion. She allowed Tasha and Nicole to take care of Logan while she stayed locked in her bedroom getting high when she wasn't suffering from morning sickness.

"I ain't scared. He family," Linda told the nurse. "Don't worry. We feed Logan on paper plates and he don't use the bathroom upstairs."

Months passed and as Logan's health continued to decline, Linda listened to the street stories about AIDS.

"What about the baby?" Logan's nurse asked again.

"I got an appointment at Burgdorf clinic," Linda confirmed. "My back's hurting me."

Linda was eight months pregnant when she finally showed up at the clinic for prenatal care. The doctor came into the examining room with a frightful look on his face. Linda covered the needle marks on her arms, but it wasn't difficult for the doctor to see that Linda was an addict. He asked her to submit to testing for tuberculosis, Hepatitis A and B and HIV, all viruses she might have contracted from sharing dirty needles with other addicts.

"You might have AIDS," he said. "It's time you start taking care of yourself and this baby." The doctor was a jolly man with a belly shaped like Santa Claus.

"What's wrong?" she whined. "Do I have herpes?"

The quizzical look on the doctor's face worried her. He explained that the pus in her back was a staph infection that had covered her spine. Her condition was serious. Linda flinched when the doctor told the nurses to hook her up to an IV, so she could receive antibiotics.

She hardly had any usable veins, she said later. That needle prick hurt worse than delivering Samantha. She weighed 5 pounds and 13 ounces at birth, three more pounds than Linda gained during her entire pregnancy. Samantha shared her parents' deep chocolate complexion and almond-shaped eyes. It was an easy delivery, but afterward Linda felt like electricity was shooting through her veins as the doctors tried to treat her infection. She asked Alvin to bring her some dope and he helped her skin-pop the heroin behind the hospital curtain to ease the discomfort she felt.

Linda returned to drinking and drugging after she left the hospital with her newborn. She didn't consider the consequences. The pain of the life she had led was too tough to deal with without self-medicating herself with heroin and alcohol.

CHAPTER 16 | AIDS

TWO YEARS PASSED BEFORE LINDA WENT BACK to the clinic in 1985. She pulled a nurse aside and asked her a question rarely requested from patients in the poor sections of Hartford.

"I need one of them AIDS tests. My girls need one, too."

Very few people in the mid-1980s voluntarily asked to be tested for HIV, which even in the medical community was considered a kiss of death. The nurse's reaction to her request frightened Linda, and she told the nurse that she wasn't leaving without getting a test for herself and her daughters. She needed to know if she had given her daughters the virus, or if they had contracted it from Logan or someone else in the family.

"Mrs. Jordan, do you understand what this is all about?" the nurse said.

"Yeah!"

Linda collected her girls from the waiting room and the nurse directed them to follow her through a long hallway, down the stairs, into the basement and through a door with a bright red "Exit" sign overhead. "Com' on," Linda said, when her girls tried turning around. They followed the nurse through one corridor and into another. When the girls questioned Linda about

where they were going, she beckoned them with her index finger to continue following the nurse. Linda prepared herself to
defuse the drama she anticipated once they made it inside the
AIDS clinic.

She asked the nurse to take her blood first in front of the
girls. Linda hated needles that were not filled with heroin and it
hurt like hell when the nurse took blood from her vein. But she
didn't flinch. "No sweat," she lied.

Tasha, Nicole and Samantha watched in horror as Linda
rolled back down her sleeve and beckoned Tasha to step up.
Linda's girls hated getting shots during their regular doctor's
visits and they cried, screamed and shook as a nurse took blood
from each of them. The nurse told Linda that the test results for
the family would be available in about a month.

"You should come back then. We offer counseling," the
nurse said as she watched Linda and the children head toward
the door. "We'll call you in."

Linda phoned the clinic every day for weeks. The social
worker refused to report the family's HIV test results without
seeing her first. Linda begrudgingly went back to the clinic, and
she was relieved when she was told that the test results were
negative. None of them had the virus.

"Thank God," Linda said as she briskly walked down the
corridor. Her family had all dodged a date with death. But the
process was stressful on the entire family. It showed the most
in ten-year-old Tasha, who resented being forced into the role
as caretaker of her younger sisters, Nicole and baby Samantha,
while Linda stayed locked in her bedroom. Tasha saw Tanya go

through the same sort of woman-child blues that had affected all the older girls in her family for generations. She hated that sort of responsibility of caring for her younger sisters while her mother partied.

Tasha had felt a sense of freedom when she was allowed to play outside with the other girls from the neighborhood. Those kinds of days were rare after Tanya had her baby and left home at age sixteen to stay with one of Linda's sisters. On one particular day, Tasha slipped outside to join a game of double-dutch. She jumped rope like her life depended upon it, despite the fact that her mother was simmering inside over an incident the night before. Nicole and a boy from the neighborhood had set a mattress on fire. The neighbors smelled smoke and called the fire department. Tasha was supposed to be watching Nicole, so she admitted to setting the blaze.

"Tasha!" Linda yelled from her bedroom window. "Get yo ass back in this damn house."

Tasha heard trouble in Linda's voice but she kept jumping rope and pretended not to hear her. None of her neighbors who dished out generous accolades about her style and speed warned Tasha that Linda had left the apartment and was marching up behind her. Before Tasha knew it, Linda had grabbed her by the neck and started dragging her toward the front porch. An older woman who was watching stopped in Linda's path. Tasha thanked God that she had been saved. She got up from the ground and rushed inside and picked up the telephone.

"Mommy tried to kill me," Tasha said to the 911 operator before she noticed that Linda was standing behind her in her nightgown with her hands on her hips.

"I'm whooping yo' ass," Linda yelled. "I don't give a damn who you done called."

The operator was still on the telephone so Tasha became brazen with her complaint. "My Mommy is losing it," Tasha said. "She beat me up for setting a fire last night. I didn't set the fire but she hit me with a broom 'cause I wasn't cleaning up the house fast enough this morning. She drunk."

"Is there any place you can go?" the 911 operator asked.

"Thelma," Tasha said, but the operator recorded the name "Dolma" in her notes for the police department records.

Tasha wrapped her hands around the telephone receiver and refused to put it down, even after Linda yanked the cord out of the wall. Linda heard sirens outside her apartment and Tasha dropped the cord.

Linda was upset that Tasha had invited that kind of drama back into her house. She exploded when she heard the police officer banging on her front door.

"Pack your fucking bags!" Linda yelled as she opened the door.

"Yeah, I hit her," she told the police officer. "Get her out of here!"

"Ah, Mommy. Please," Tasha begged.

"Calm down," said the police officer. He was stunned that Linda hadn't tried to defuse the situation. Her profanity was exacerbating the problem.

The police officer understood once Linda told him why she was so stressed out.

"I just had a baby and I can't depend upon Tasha and Nicole to help me hold it down around the house," Linda told the officer. "Them girls cause a lot of trouble for me. They set a mattress on fire upstairs last night. Now my landlord say we got to go."

But the officer lost his empathy for Linda once he looked deeply into her eyes and recognized the classic signs of someone who had too much to drink. He examined Tasha. There were no bruises on her face, arms or neck, so he left the apartment.

He reported the incident at the end of his shift to his supervisor, who reported it to the city's welfare office. Another abuse complaint wouldn't help Linda when she sought help from her social worker finding another apartment. The ten years she had spent living at 97D Van Block Avenue in the Kings housing project was coming to an end.

Before the end of the week, her social worker received a message from a mysterious caller who said Linda was selling drugs out of her apartment. The caller said there was no food in the house and Linda had allowed strangers to sleep on her couch and throughout her apartment. The caller covered the mouthpiece over the telephone to disguise his or her voice and belted out inflammatory allegations that made every social worker in the office who heard the message come to attention. The caller said that Linda had allowed a man to point a loaded gun at her children; her smallest children played with used needles; and all types of sexual acts were performed in front of the children.

Linda was unaware that the caller had made those outrageous claims to the welfare worker that April in 1987. She only knew that she had to move because she had not paid her rent.

Samantha, Linda's youngest daughter, opened the door when Miss Dayner, the family's new social worker, stopped by for a visit the following afternoon. "Is your mother home?

"She sleep."

"Please, I need to see her."

Samantha wrestled Linda awake and told her that a worker was at the door. Linda looked disheveled when she showed up at the door and was wiping sleep from her eyes.

"I need a place to stay," Linda said.

There were more pressing issues to deal with first, Miss Dayner told Linda. She asked to see all of Linda's children. Tasha, Nicole and Samantha were shabbily dressed in wrinkled T-shirts and panties as they filed down the stairs. Their hair hadn't been combed. Linda noticed that her children looked unkempt.

"They getting ready for their baths," Linda lied.

Linda admitted unwittingly that she had forgotten to get her oldest daughters dressed for school. Alongside the girls was a little boy wearing a wet diaper.

"And who is this little one?" the social worker asked.

"That's Tanya's son, John," Linda said. "My grandson."

"I guess you know why I'm here," Miss Dayner continued. "This isn't the first time, Mrs. Jordan, that the police have reported that you lost control of yourself around your children. But I'm here to investigate another complaint of a more serious nature."

"What lies you listening to now?" Linda asked.

The worker rattled off the laundry list of allegations that she had heard over the office's answering machine.

"Lies and more lies," Linda said. "That was a toy gun. I'll show you."

Linda returned from upstairs holding a fake black handgun. The social worker flinched when she saw how real it looked.

"Come see," Linda said as she walked into the kitchen. It was spotless and smelled of bleach and Lysol. Linda opened the refrigerator door so the worker could see the eggs, bacon and packages of bologna and cheese for the girls' lunches. The cabinets were stocked with cereals and canned foods.

"Lies, I told you," Linda said.

Before Miss Dayner could respond, Linda interrupted the social worker. She was new to her job, and Linda was a master at manipulating social workers who hadn't done their homework.

"I'm tired of ya'll telling me how to raise these bad ass kids of mine. Hell yeah, I smacked Tasha down. I'll do it again if she talks back, sets another fire or misbehaves," Linda said.

Miss Dayner took copious notes as Linda rattled off all of the violations that could lead to her losing her children.

"You have a baby and three other daughters," Miss Dayner said carefully. "Getting angry now won't solve this. Linda, your anger is becoming a problem. Have you considered getting some help? Some counseling."

"Problem?" Linda yelled. "I'm not the problem. Okay! Them bad ass kids is the damn problem."

Her conversation with Linda had deteriorated. Miss Dayner wrote in her report that all of Linda's problems might be solved if she agreed to parenting and anger management classes. She cited Linda's alcoholism and her inability to discipline 12-year-old Tasha without being physically abusive.

"Mother feels strongly that she wants Tasha to fear her, and that she'll beat her anytime she feels that the child deserves it," the official report said. Miss Dayner recommended to her supervisor later that day that Tasha should stay with relatives until Linda cooled down. But after reading Linda's voluminous file late at work that night, she changed her mind and recommended that Tasha might be better served if she went to a group home. Linda was right about a few things, Miss Dayner thought. Tasha needed a structured home life. There was no guarantee that she could get proper parenting with Linda's family.

The decision to send Tasha away was not immediate. It took more than a year for the social workers to secure a bed for her at the home for troubled girls. In the meantime, Linda's relationship with Tasha continued to deteriorate. But she had more pressing issues on her mind. A nurse from the clinic had demanded that she attend a counseling session at the AIDS clinic. When she arrived, the social worker from the health department said that Linda had tested positive for HIV after her second test in 1989. The crushing news drove Linda back to her bed. She got high for the next three days.

When Miss Dayner called again, Linda agreed to voluntarily give up her parental rights to Tasha.

"Tasha! Pack your bags," Linda yelled once she got off the telephone.

"What?" Tasha said as a tear fell down her face.

"Pack your bags. You wanted out of here when you called the police on me. Didn't you?" Linda said. "Get your shit!"

"But Mommy?" Tasha protested. She never expected Linda to give her up so easily.

"Pack your bags. They found a bed for you outside of Hartford in a place called Warehouse Point."

Tasha resented Linda at that moment. She promised herself that she would tell the social worker about her mother's heroin habit to get back at her. She smiled when she noticed that Linda's landlord had slapped another eviction notice on the door of the apartment. "That's what she get," Tasha said when she saw Linda pull the notice off the front door.

"Damn," Linda cursed in a voice loud enough to wake the dead.

Tasha backed out of Linda's reach. She felt tempted to reach out to her mother later that day to give her a hug, but her own feelings of rejection overpowered her. She felt like jumping rope with her friends from the Kings, but she stayed inside and washed her clothes and hung them around the house to dry.

"If she don't want me, I'm outta here," Tasha told seven-year-old Nicole, who looked scared, abandoned and angry.

"Don't worry, little sistah," Tasha said. "I'll be okay."

Tasha crossed her fingers over her heart so Nicole knew she meant it.

"I got you. No matter what Linda does. Just take care of baby girl Sam."

Behind the scenes, a supervisor in Miss Dayner office transferred Linda's abuse file to a more seasoned social worker. The office received another report from Linda's property manager, who confirmed that "drug dealing is going on in the apartment and the children have been made to sleep in the basement while mother has drug parties." Linda was being evicted, the manager said. "I'm doing this for the children."

The office of the state Department of Children and Families went into high alert. The social workers there didn't wait to figure out what to do next. Within a day, Miss Toledano, a firm and decisive social worker with more experience, was placed in charge of the new investigation. Linda knew immediately that the social worker didn't play once a friend from her children's school called to say that her new social worker was asking a lot of questions.

Miss T, as Linda called her, had covered all of her bases. She had read every page of Linda's history before she showed up for an unexpected visit. She knew that Tasha had made a fake report but sensed that Linda wasn't being a good parent. Good parents would never willingly send one of their children away to a home for troubled girls. Conscientious mothers argued and fought to keep their children.

Linda looked haggard when Miss T knocked on her door. She hadn't washed or dressed when she answered the door and allowed the social worker inside her apartment. The younger children were dirty and unkempt, and the worker suspected that alcohol wasn't Linda's only addiction.

Before Miss T processed the paperwork needed for Linda to relinquish her parental rights for Tasha, someone put a slip of paper on her desk. Someone at Mount Sinai Hospital reported that Linda's breath smelled of liquor when she brought Nicole to the hospital for her asthma treatment. Miss T didn't know that Linda was battling a new demon called HIV.

Tasha's departure took longer than anyone in the family expected. Linda's cousin Logan passed out in her basement. She brought him upstairs by herself and waited impatiently on the ambulance. Tasha had refused to help, and Linda attacked Tasha with a broom. She ended up in the hospital with Logan. The welts on her back were proof enough that Tasha needed to be removed from the home.

Linda sent her other two girls to live with her sisters after Tasha left for Warehouse Point. She locked herself in her bedroom with her favorite companions, a spoon, a candle, a needle filled with heroin, and a bottle of rum.

She was in the bedroom one day when Alvin kicked in the door. He had picked the front door lock to get into the apartment. Though they had divorced, Linda and Alvin continued to party together. He stayed at her place when he wasn't staying with his sister.

"You ain't the only one around here who likes to party," he said.

Linda didn't fight off Alvin when he joined her on the mattress. They partied together until they ran out of dope. They discussed what Linda would do once she lost her apartment and a probate judge officially allowed her to sign their children away. They weren't winnable issues, Linda thought. She felt defeated, but with Alvin by her side, she felt that she might be able to convince the judge that together they could keep their youngest children. Without them, The Welfare would cut off Linda's food stamps and her monthly check.

She sold her TV, record player and toaster so she could buy herself a new suit at the thrift store and hits of heroin to tide them over until their court day. Linda saved enough money to give Alvin a buck or two because he had been a workhorse around the house. She needed help packing her belongings and cleaning the apartment. The housing court had commissioned a sheriff to put her things out on the street. She was tempted to retire back to her room when the blues tried to take over, but pressed on until all of her belongings were in boxes. She figured she could sell everything else if she needed a fix.

Linda had spent years binging on drugs and alcohol since her first HIV test. She had lost her girls, and was about to be homeless once she stopped paying for her fifty-dollar-a-night room at a motel on the Berlin Turnpike. She expected to die soon once she began noticing that many folks she had gotten high with had begun wasting away from AIDS.

Alvin was hospitalized toward the end of the month. He went through a battery of tests that showed he had weak lungs, was HIV positive and needed bed rest. After 28 days of antibiotics, steroids and narcotics, the doctors sent him on his way with a warning that he had an infectious disease. Linda was ready to die with Alvin. She overdosed more than once and cursed God each time she was revived.

She didn't think she had much to live for once her daughter Tanya got hooked on cocaine. The thought of Tanya's addiction made Linda want to stop getting high, but she didn't know how. Somebody had told her about going to the methadone clinic if she wanted to kick her habit, but she substituted heroin for bottles of cheap rum to take off the edge. She showed up drunk at the foster home where the younger girls lived. Their foster mother, Mrs. Bea, told her never to come back to her home in that condition.

"You drunk?" Beatrice Wilburn said as she hung clothes out on the line. "Come to church on Sunday if you want to see them. You ain't welcome round here like this."

"Church?" Linda said. "I ain't been. I don't go to church."

"Everybody is welcome," Mrs. Bea said as she wrung out her children's clothes on the line. "That's the only place to be if you wanna see them."

Linda wasn't comfortable attending Sunday church service with a monkey on her back. After Alvin got arrested again for stealing heroin from a dealer, she was alone in the world. Bottles of rum became Linda's drug of choice. But she missed getting high on heroin.

CHAPTER 17 | STEPS

WHEN LINDA WAS A CHILD, tales of heroin's purity swept through the streets with the speed of ghetto folklore. Once Vietnam veterans came home bragging about how heroin was the great equalizer of all the painful things they had heard, seen and felt in the war, abused and forgotten people living in the overcrowded housing projects of this insurance capital got hooked on the powerful narcotic. It wasn't hard for drug dealers to penetrate this mid-sized city between Beantown and the Big Apple. Linda got caught up in it when she ventured down into the basement with her girlfriend to see what all the fuss was about. Linda was always curious about the tales of the soothing powers of the fabled white powder. Her curiosity directed her down this crooked path foretold in the Scriptures.

But now, Linda's heroin habit was exacting a special kind of pain after decades of traveling down this road. Once she found out that she was HIV positive, she didn't care anymore. She showed just how low she could go to get a bag full of nickels for her next hit. If she were going to die, she might as well end this period of purgatory. She stayed determined, on a mission toward death, once Logan, Alvin's cousin, could no longer walk and she saw how much of a dirty dog this disease could be.

Without her children or a place to stay, she had to hustle to go to a distant place in her mind that brought her comfort. The crooked journey foretold in the books of Isaiah and Luke left her wounded as she traveled aimlessly down city blocks unaware of how she looked or smelled. She felt that death might tap her on the shoulder any day. She didn't know whether the disease would one day rob her of all of her bodily functions, as it had done Logan, or if her next hit of heroin would be her last. Her mind was on the latter when one of God's angels gently placed his hand on her shoulder and shook her back into reality.

"Linda! Linda!" the voice echoed. "Don't you want something better for yourself?"

Linda didn't need to turn around to know she was busted while fishing through trash cans for returned bottles. She felt naked and unkempt as she combed her thin, straight black locks into place with her fingers. She couldn't think of what to say, so she put her thumb in her mouth, a habit that gave her comfort as a child.

"Com' on, Linda. Stop that," the voice behind her begged. "Let me take you to get some help."

"Ah, Daddy," Linda said.

"Ah, Daddy, nothing. I heard it all before. Let me take you."

"Take me?" Linda pulled away.

"I'll get my car."

They had had the same conversation for years, but today Daddy Harry, her real daddy, was not taking no for an answer. She considered for a second what she was up against if she wasn't ready to go into treatment.

"Not today," said Linda, breaking into a sprint and hiding behind a building.

"I'll be back. I'm not giving up. Ya hear me!" Harry yelled, something a dignified man like him didn't do much. "Damn, Linda. Why don't you come on?"

Linda knew that Harry wanted to see her go to treatment much more than she wanted it. She didn't have the heart to tell him that she wasn't ready. Treatment was a gamble. She had rolled that set of dice over the course of years, four or five times before. Just getting a bed would be a drag. The staff behind the locked door of the center she called "The Blues" had too many rules and the workers there asked too many questions.

"How long have you been strung out?" the treatment center attendant might ask. "Who do you get high with? Where did you cop your last fix?"

She had heard that mantra from the treatment worker before. The intake worker's questions gave her an itch that she couldn't scratch. She walked away that time hurling biting insults.

"Ya'll need to rewrite that damn script," Linda quipped the last time she let Harry talk her into going into treatment. "You sound like the police," Linda yelled as she headed for the outer door.

Daddy Harry knew the doctor in charge of the clinic and he had once served on the treatment center's board. The first two times, Linda had stayed a few days. But she wasn't ready to give up her addictions. Once, when Daddy Harry caught Linda at home in the Kings in the latter part of 1985, she was too intoxicated to sit up. Nicole and Samantha were running around the house half naked and they didn't have on any shoes. It was wintertime.

When Harry found Linda wandering the streets four years later, he lost his temper. He grabbed her by the arm and wouldn't let go. Linda was dirty, high and drunk.

"You hurtin' me," Linda said looking up into her father's eyes.

Harry had never put his hands on her and he startled her when he picked her up. What was he doing? She tried kicking her legs against his six foot, four inch frame. Linda nearly tripped as he threw her into the car. She knew instantly where he was taking her. The Blue Hills Treatment Center was nearby and he probably had reserved a spot for her. This time, four years later, she knew she would cave in if she went into treatment for anyone other than herself.

"You are going to have to go," Harry said.

"I need help," Linda said, no longer defiant. "I want to stop. I do. Let me do it."

"I want to go with you," Harry said. "But I can't. You are going to need to do it for yourself. I love you, Linda. I want you to do better."

Linda believed him. She didn't know if she was ready to wrestle with her demons.

"You can do this," Harry said.

"I'm going to stay this time," Linda said as she walked in the front door of the treatment center. She recognized the place and didn't look back. The attendant sitting behind the glass window looked up from his newspaper and inspected Linda's appearance. Her addictions were obvious.

"Name and Social Security card ... When was the last time you used? ... Where do you cop your dope?" the man peppered her with rapid-fire questions.

Linda lost it. She pulled out a pocketknife that she carried when she bought dope from strangers and waved it toward the glass partition between them.

"Enough!" Linda yelled. "Let me end this now. You can clean up the mess. Okay!"

Linda had positioned the blade on her neck before the attendant jumped to his feet, unlocked the door and opened the door for Linda. He knew a serious suicide attempt when he saw one.

What happened next was a blur to Linda. She woke up sitting on a cot in a locked concrete room that reminded her of a jail cell. She cried for mercy as she tossed and turned inside the room. She was left alone to wrestle the demons that revealed themselves during her daydreams and nightmares.

The heroin withdrawal robbed Linda of her bodily fluids for five excruciating days. The flashbacks she saw reminded her of every bad thing she had experienced since she was five years old. Her personal Mary Seacole changed her bedpan when she needed it. Linda initially ignored her words of comfort, but the woman believed in taking care of her patients. She had seen Linda at the center before, so this time when Linda was lucid enough to ask for a shower, she spent time at her bedside.

"I'm here for you," said the nurse, who explained how the

treatment center worked. She told Linda to expect more sleepless nights and horrific dreams as the drugs worked their way out of her system. Your hallucinations were based upon true memories, the nurse said.

"The worst part is over. We've got meetings. Going to them might help," she said.

"Meetings?" Linda asked sarcastically.

"You don't have to talk if you don't want, but you should share. They say talking in those meetings help. There's a lot of love and a lot of misery that's going to come out of you before the healing begins. Don't worry about the other patients telling your business. Everything said in our meetings is kept secret and stays within the group. You'll see that your journey is like the journeys of most addicts. All that hurt starts at home."

Linda's mind drifted off while the nurse was speaking. She wasn't trying to be rude, but she was feeling the hurt brought on by the life she had lived.

The nurse didn't expect a response. But she had a few more things she needed to tell Linda so she could prepare herself for the next twenty eight days inside the center. If you stay, attend those meetings. There are counseling sessions here, too. Your case manager will say when you are ready to go home.

"You wanna go home, don't you?"

Linda hadn't felt at home since the time she lived in her first apartment, when she was a teenager. She had burned so many bridges with her family before coming to Blue Hills that she wasn't sure they'd make a place for her once she was released.

"I ain't got no home," Linda whispered.

"Don't worry about all that now. Just start slowly. They call it taking steps here. When you reach the twelfth step you'll know it. Start slowly. Take one step at a time," the nurse said.

Her time passed quickly. From the detoxification ward, Linda was allowed to move around freely to other parts of the center. She was pleased to learn that she could go into the courtyard to smoke cigarettes when she had them. She saw signs posted in the corridors about the meetings her intake nurse had told her about.

The nurse's instructions became her guide. Every hour on the hour somebody was talking about one of those meetings. The nurses, patients and social workers were always chatting about them when the announcements were broadcast over the speakers at meal times.

Linda was reluctant but curious. There was something scary about sharing intimate details about her life with strangers. She took a seat in one of the card table chairs in the back row. She looked around the room and recognized some of the faces. Her body language was stiff and guarded as she folded her arms around her chest, a familiar sign to the group's seasoned members that she was new to the meetings.

After everyone was seated, the group leaders passed out clipboards with the phrase "12 Step Program" printed in big block letters. Many of the people in Linda's row declined to take a board and they passed them down the line. Linda didn't take one either because she wasn't sure what the 12 Step Program meant, but she wished she had once the group starting reciting in unison the mantra created for Narcotics Anonymous and Alcoholics Anonymous recovery programs.

"We admitted we were powerless over alcohol that our lives had become unmanageable. Came to believe that a Power greater than ourselves could restore us to sanity ..."

Linda couldn't keep up after the first lines. The words "powerless" and "unmanageable" stuck out in her mind. Her eyes moistened listening to people in the group as they told stories about how they were abused and neglected as children. Their stories made her mind drift to those secret places that she had tried to hide for so many years.

She didn't speak that first time. But later in the quiet of her bedroom, she grew agitated because she couldn't stop daydreaming. Her mind darkened every time someone at the center mentioned the words "addictions" and "recovery." She didn't quite understand what recovery meant, but she thought about trying to find out what it meant if it would stop the visions flickering inside her mind like a burning candle, even after she had closed her eyes at night. This went on for weeks until a psychologist explained that her recovery would never start if she didn't open up and come to grips with the painful memories she had buried deep inside.

The meetings became her new addiction.

"Do you know why you use heroin?" her psychologist asked bluntly during a counseling session.

"Yeah," Linda said.

"Why?"

"Because of what they did to me," Linda said as she put her head down.

She could no longer conceal the shame she felt for not being able to handle her memories of abuse.

"They?"

"They molested, beat and raped me," Linda said of her family. "I must of loved him, I married him twice."

"You said they. Who are they?"

"Before Alvin, my granddaddy took advantage of me," Linda said. "My mommy beat me too, so, she could keep me quiet."

Linda's memories were taking shape. She shared all the painful things that she had kept to herself with anyone who would listen. She began repeating her story of how her life was shaped by traumatic experiences, and how her growth was stunted when she medicated herself with alcohol and heroin as a teenager. She took her first drink when she was twelve. Linda hadn't planned on telling her psychologist about her buried memories, but she couldn't stop herself when she came to grips with the dramatic events that had shaped her life. She thought about every intimate detail each night when she laid her head on the hard pillow and slept, perhaps peacefully for the first time since she was a little girl.

Her captivating stories of rape, molestation and physical abuse became the focal points of her group meetings. She wanted to glamorize her experiences, but found no need once she started speaking. It was a good thing, too. The experienced addicts in her recovery group could smell out a bullshit story. They urged Linda to face the realities of what it meant to have traveled down a crooked road. After a while, her voice stopped quivering during the difficult parts of her story, especially the times when she wanted to make Alvin, who left her alone as a teenage mother to raise their babies, seem like a better person than he was.

Anger rose up inside of Linda as she reconciled that she had used drugs and alcohol to cover up the pain that he and others had caused when they stole her innocence. Her peers, the group leaders and professionals listened in speechless awe. They weren't used to hearing a person so new to recovery revealing parts of herself that so many others were ashamed to share.

Linda found it easier and easier to take the microphone. Some of the members in her group groaned when she stood up to speak. It wasn't that the other addicts didn't respect her revelations but her truthfulness made them feel small by comparison. Her honesty exposed the fact that they had not explored their own demons. They were also afraid that those who couldn't resist gossiping about what Linda had shared with others outside of the group might violate the confidentiality rules. Linda insisted for weeks that she had more to share and that she hadn't revealed her most precious secret, a skeleton in her trove of revelations that had the potential to propel her out of the locked ward and back into the streets where she could easily "pick up heroin" for another fix.

"I'm HIV positive," Linda said at one meeting.

The room went silent.

"That's what I've been hiding from ya'll. It is my secret and I can't hide from the virus no more. I'm not ready to die anymore. I'd be gone by now if I was going to be taken out by this disease. I'm ready to live."

Everyone in the room had secrets, but Linda had shared

something that even made the social workers and professionals nervous. Everyone in the room stopped moving. Some of them didn't know enough at that time about the disease to know if they were in danger. They couldn't say for sure how the disease was spread. They wanted to run out of the room, but Linda's words kept them fixed to their seats.

"Don't worry. I'm not dying. I'm going to live with this thang," Linda said. "God is going to let me live long enough so I can help others."

The HIV virus was very scary to almost everyone in the room. Linda didn't know whether her last statement was true, but she believed it nevertheless. The group recognized Linda's courage and willed themselves not to shy away from her. Trained professionals at the treatment center who prided themselves on maintaining the confidentiality of their clients couldn't help talking about how Linda had announced her HIV status. The staff hadn't heard a heterosexual woman from the African-American community willing to admit that she had the virus. They braced themselves behind closed doors about the consequences of what Linda had made public.

Their worries were abated when Linda's stock rose to the level of celebrity in the HIV and Narcotics Anonymous communities. The coordinators of the treatment programs no longer looked at Linda as a down-and-out addict. They invited her to other meetings outside of the center, where she was asked to share aspects of her story with professionals who had read the statistics from the U.S. Centers for Disease Control and Prevention about a growing population among drug-addicted black women with the virus, but who had never met anyone willing to tell their story. Her openness was overwhelming to most of them but they saw Linda as a beacon and a new light in HIV/AIDS prevention.

The professionals brought their clients from outside the center and lined the rooms of Linda's regular meetings to hear what Linda had to say. Her story wasn't different from a typical female addict who was abused as a child. Those kinds of stories were common and overexposed.

Linda talked about the consequences of being a drug-addicted mother who hadn't shown signs of the new virus but still embraced it. Even Linda didn't know why she was sharing so much. This fearless step of sharing her story made Linda dig deeper into her heart for the source of her emotional pain during her private counseling sessions. She shared intimate details with her therapist about what her granddaddy had done to her. She talked about how she was ignored when she cried out in pain and how dope became her best friend during difficult times in her life.

Recovery was tricky. Though Linda had confronted her demons in public, her memories haunted her when everything was quiet late at night. She imagined going to the gravesite of her grandfather and excavating his body. Thoughts of her lost and neglected childhood showed Linda why she had followed in the footsteps of her mother Edith, who drank herself to death. Her mother's alcoholism had made her unaware of the needs of this middle child and had helped to destroy her emotional health. If she could, she thought it might also be wise to dig up her mother, too. She imagined having conversations with her dead mother and grandparents so she could ask them why they had mistreated her so. She wanted to have the same conversation with Alvin, but she was certain that he wouldn't listen.

Linda's revelations empowered others in her women's-only group who recognized the liberating force of what Linda had done for them. Their tears were small tokens of appreciation. As black women they had all suffered in silence and used alcohol, drugs and prostitution to cover up the injuries hemorrhaging inside. But she was the only one of them in the beginning to reveal her HIV status.

"I would dig up my granddaddy if I could dig," Linda told the group once she reconciled the goals for her recovery. "I'd forgive him if it would help me move on with my life. I would forgive them all."

That revelation liberated her of the guilt she had carried with her for nearly thirty years like a heavy load. She hadn't realized that she also had to forgive herself if she were to get better. Linda's psychologist saw her progress and told her after three months of treatment that she was ready to restart her life drug free outside the locked doors of the center. The counselors wanted Linda to win in her recovery, but they also preached the familiar edict that "once an addict, always an addict." They promised her that her new life would be harder than her difficult past. She would need to develop a new way of thinking and would need to stop herself from manipulating when it was convenient. Otherwise, the guilt that she had harbored would return and feed upon her emotions and lack of self-esteem.

"You can do this, Linda," her psychologist said.

"Yeah, I know," she said.

CHAPTER 18 | LIFE SAVER

LINDA FELT LIKE A RELEASED PRISONER once she breathed in the fresh air the first time she stepped outside of the locked ward at Blue Hills. She felt ready to start her new life, but nothing prepared her for the recognition that the city of her birth, one populated by drug dealers and addicts, could be her worst enemy.

She vowed to reverse her course by divorcing herself from her old ways. But mantras like that are just words. Particular neighborhoods and housing projects triggered memories of Linda traveling down basement stairs and into back alleys where she used to party with friends and family. The promises she made to herself vanished as she plotted on where she'd need to go for a taste of liquor and a tiny bit of heroin. Her mind, the most powerful bodily organ, was playing tricks on her and she hadn't left the sidewalk in front of the center. She immediately wanted to walk back inside.

"There were too many people in Hartford doing dope or scheming to get dope. And liquor flows across this city like a bootlegger's spigot," she told a worker at the desk who looked puzzled when Linda walked back inside and dropped her bag on the floor.

When she finally left, Linda decided against staying with family during her first few months outside of treatment. She accepted a bed in a halfway house across the street from the clinic. She stayed there until she learned the boundaries of maintaining her recovery. She had vowed to walk down a new road and she hoped to avoid the roadblocks she confronted each time she went outside. She didn't tell her family where she was staying, but word seeped out to her relatives who thought that being in treatment for ninety days should have been enough for Linda to get on with her life. They had no clue what Linda had gone through or where she was headed.

Staying in Stowe Village, a notorious federal housing project named after the famous author Harriett Beecher Stowe, was initially out of the question. She knew where drug dealers and addicts shacked up inside the red-brick buildings where hundreds of Hartford's most impoverished residents and suburbanites got their dope. The drug traffic in "The Vil" was so heavy that it drew the attention of investigators from the DEA, FBI and state and local cops. It was an easy place "to pick up" and Linda stayed away from the complex as much as she could.

Linda focused her attention on her new obsessions, plotting ways to get her children back and going to as many Narcotics Anonymous meetings as she could. She learned from other drug-addicted single mothers in those meetings how to stay off dope and to "work her recovery."

For Linda that meant she had to be selfish about every aspect of her self-discovery. She knew she would never be whole again until she got her girls back and she couldn't do that until she was free of her past addictions. Other women in her group also had lost their children, and they shared a bond with Linda. Though it was hard to admit, their addictions were greater than their love for their children.

Linda asked her counselor at the treatment center and other professionals for help finding a permanent place to stay that was suitable to the folks down at The Welfare. The health care professionals at the center were eager to help Linda, but they had other motives. They needed a recovering addict who wasn't afraid to share her HIV status at fundraisers. They needed money for their AIDS and HIV prevention programs, and Linda was successfully placing a human face on the growing statistic of African-American women in the early 1990s that were just starting to live with the virus. Women like Linda hadn't shown up at ACT-UP rallies, AIDS quilt memorials and candlelight vigils until now.

Linda accepted a job as a part-time outreach worker at one of the programs. She felt comfortable distributing condoms to prostitutes and bleach kits to the addicts, but she was afraid of the administrative part of the job. Her language skills reflected her poor education and she was intimidated when she was asked to write about her reflections of the day, a skill she hadn't yet acquired.

Program coordinators at different agencies heard about Linda's speedy recovery and her new vocation. They figured that Linda's presence at AIDS prevention board meetings in predominately white communities might allow those programs to compete for grants that the Urban League and Latinas Contras SIDA, groups catering to underprivileged black and Hispanic communities, were getting from the government. Using regular people of color who were HIV positive as outreach workers was a new strategy among HIV/AIDS prevention programs.

Linda stepped up when others facing similar circumstances continued to hide their HIV status from their families, friends and the general public. Despite the encouragement of her new friends and mentors, the new path that Linda had chosen wasn't easy and she felt insecure working a white-collar job. She was used to getting her hands dirty digging potatoes, cleaning office buildings, doing factory work and risking her liberty when she sold drugs and hosted gambling parties to feed her habit and her family.

She started accepting offers to speak at small engagements a few times a month. The various organizations paid for her transportation and gave her a small stipend for other expenses. She liked that kind of job. Her powerful life story was compelling enough to attract donors from outside the AIDS community who wanted to fund outreach programs. Linda was not only an outreach worker but also a resource for the professionals at different organizations who didn't know much about people with her life experiences. They gave her a seat in their boardrooms and she gladly sat at the table and ate the free food.

But Linda refused to get caught up in her new celebrity status. She kept herself grounded by keeping her ties to the original members of her treatment center group. The women there often reminded Linda that relapse was also a part of her recovery, and if she got a big head she might end up back to treatment in a locked ward.

Once the AIDS organizations began marketing Linda's story, she told influential leaders who led AIDS funding into Hartford's HIV community that she needed financial vouchers for new housing, and stipends for her electricity, telephone, heat and water bills, before she could successfully petition a probate judge for visitation and custody of Samantha, Nicole and Tasha. She had given her daughters up voluntarily, and that worked in her favor as her hearings progressed through the court.

Linda was surprised when her new friends, who had come from different educational backgrounds, showed up in court to support her. She didn't know if they felt sorry for her. But she appreciated their presence because she could bypass the social workers who looked down on her once they reviewed the voluminous files of her history with The Welfare. The thousands of pages of opened and closed child abuse reports, they thought, could not be ignored.

Linda remained a persistent hustler at heart. She refused to give up. She stayed at the halfway house but accepted rides to the other side of town to meet her social workers and to visit her children. Her outreach work also required her to go back into neighborhoods she feared. She imagined sometimes that she was once again traveling down a crooked road. Linda told her friends who gave her rides to appointments that joining the real world came with an irresistible temptation to get high.

"I'm not sure I'm ready," Linda told a friend.

"You know what they say," her friend and sponsor responded.

"Yeah, I know. Take one step at a time," Linda said. She pressed her face against the car window and looked at Hartford through sober eyes. She felt as if she were a stranger. She didn't know her place as a sober woman. Most of the people she had associated with before she became serious about her sobriety had lived in a perpetual state of intoxication. Treatment had taught her to breathe and to take baby steps, but just traveling through the streets of the poor and depressed city hurt her heart.

The crack and heroin addicts had taken over familiar parts of the city and left blighted buildings and despair behind. So many people like her had given up or never dreamed of living better lives, Linda thought. She didn't judge them. She stayed on her new path because it was the only way to regain custody of her daughters.

The professionals she had met were trying to mold Linda into an icon in the AIDS community here and across the nation. "Coping with your stress will be the hardest part, if you are confident and continue to fight the system for your girls," her friend said during the ride.

"I'm clean now," Linda said boldly as she got out of the car.

She walked into The Welfare office with that same confidence until she was greeted by her newest social worker. She had heard about Linda, read her files and wasn't convinced when Linda told her she had changed. The woman judged Linda with her eyes.

"Don't worry. You'll see," Linda said curtly as she did an about face toward the office door.

Linda felt rejected and it showed in her body language. She knew that she'd need to prove her social worker wrong, but it

would take time. Still, Linda told herself that her life was look-
ing up. She had already accomplished a lot by kicking her habits.
She could look at herself in the mirror as a changed woman.
Those were achievements that took her decades to reach.

Linda began going to the church her younger girls attended
on Sundays. Tasha, Nicole and Samantha, the youngest, were
always happy to see her there. But Tasha and Nicole were old
enough to remember the old Linda. They didn't trust the new
Linda who showed up at the Salvation Army mission church
wearing new clothes and with a new attitude.

The Salvationists were familiar to Linda. She remembered
them as church workers who wore blue military-style uniforms
and rang charity bells outside of the grocery stores at Christmas. Linda had mocked the bell ringers for years. Now she was
seeking help from the Wilburns: Mrs. Bea, the children's foster
mother who they called Bede, and from her husband, who the
children called Uncle Pounchy.

Linda knew the Wilburns were good people by the way they
dressed her girls, did their hair and provided them with a stable
drug-free home. Yet the couple's growing relationship with her
daughters made Linda jealous. She wanted to be angry with
them, but she couldn't once the couple showered her with reassuring smiles and small gifts as rewards for remaining sober.

Capt. Gregory Norman and his wife, the ministers at the
church, also liked Linda. They offered her donations from their
Sunday offering plates and hot meals when they found out about
her situation. They didn't judge her, something she expected
from the clergy, once they learned she was a troubled addict try-

ing to get back on her feet. When the Normans asked what they could do for her, Linda thought about something they could do for her new friends from recovery. She asked the ministers to take a risk by opening up the church's doors for regular Narcotics Anonymous and Alcoholics Anonymous meetings. She didn't ask for anything for herself but a place for her and her friends to meet closer to their homes.

The request was a test for Linda. She wanted to be assured that the Salvation Army ministers and their congregation could offer something more valuable to the community than a gym for teenagers to play basketball.

Linda joined the church once it created more outreach programs for addicts like her who were struggling with their sobriety. She quickly excelled into church leadership positions and was surprised on the day the pastor's secretary called her into the office to measure her for a new blue uniform with patches on the shoulders.

Linda felt grateful that day. She was moving up in the world and she appreciated everyone who had opened up their hearts to her and her children. She didn't discriminate when she was asked to speak at different functions. She accepted speaking engagements sponsored by whites, blacks, Hispanics, dope fiends, gays and nuns. Her leadership abilities, though limited, propelled Linda into places she had never expected to go. She spoke on college campuses, at city hall and in white churches across the state. She had found her calling and a permanent place in the AIDS prevention community once she found God and accepted Jesus Christ. Her newfound faith in God was something that she used to minister to others.

Her religious conversion was addictive in a positive way. She attended Bible studies when she wasn't going to recovery meetings. Linda wasn't ashamed of her past and it showed. Though she spoke in broken English, it didn't matter to her audiences once she started telling her story about the painful road she had taken before God showed her that HIV, for her, was a blessing.

"The virus saved my life," Linda told a room full of Trinity College students one morning in Hartford. When one young man asked how she got the virus during the beginning of that speech, Linda wasn't caught off guard.

"What does it matter?" she told him. "I can't give it back."

Linda kept her message focused because she didn't want this group of privileged white students to try to undermine her message of prevention. If she contracted the virus, they could, too, she told them.

Speeches like that helped Linda gain allies from all segments of the city and the state. She was slowly gaining attention from national groups that asked her to accept speaking engagements at conferences throughout the country. Linda considered declining those engagements because the thought of appearing before a national audience made her nervous. She felt more comfortable accepting other engagements from the leaders of the white churches, who offered her a place in their pulpits during AIDS healing services when black church leaders would not.

The ministers in her own community, with the exception of a few ministries in Hartford, New Britain and New Haven, declined Linda's offers to speak in their churches about having

HIV. Their rejection hurt Linda, but she looked at the denial in the African-American religious community as a challenge and an opportunity to establish her own ministry. Still, their rejection puzzled her. And it still hurt.

Jesus had saved and forgiven her. She knew that a cross section of the African-American community shunned former addicts with HIV despite the fact that they had sung in their choirs and sat in pews on Sundays. Her desire to change their minds became her new calling. She refused to be ignored despite her HIV status. Linda saw that the virus was rapidly robbing too many churchgoers and their families of their dignity and they were suffering in silence and shame inside church. Despite this obstacle, Linda felt confident that she was doing God's work.

Now it was time to get her family back.

CHAPTER 19 | HOPE

WHEN IT WAS TIME FOR LINDA TO SEEK PERMISSION from the court for visitations with her daughters, she moved into an apartment in Stowe Village. She sought the help of white religious leaders, nuns like Sister Peg and priests like Father Jerome, community and health workers like Gwendolyn Lewis and Femi Assegai and Gloria Austin at the Urban League, and Iris Rivera Acosta at the city health department. In their own way, they all preached and lived Liberation Theology.

Linda gravitated toward people who were outside of her class, her neighborhood and her educational background. She selected people who were sensitive to the needs of a poor black mother embracing a new life. Linda electrified them with her passion to live when others considered an HIV diagnosis a death sentence.

"Linda had changed her life," said Lewis, who coordinated AIDS programs for the state Department of Public Health. "I did everything I could to help her. I took her to speaking engagements. She was good at telling her story."

Linda's zeal for her new life with the virus spread throughout the AIDS intervention communities. Her faith was visual and the people that she surrounded herself with recognized that the power of her story, her faith and her recovery was infectious. She attached herself to these professionals because they offered her vouchers when it was time to move out on her own. The community groups and religious leaders helped Linda rent a two-bedroom apartment big enough for her girls when they visited on the weekends. She knew she had to take baby steps accepting her new lifestyle before the professionals in the city's welfare office would permanently trust her with her children.

Unexpected doors were opening behind the scenes for Linda and her family. A local group of Quakers, a historic religious organization that Linda knew nothing about, had heard about Linda's story and offered her a chance to rent a five-bedroom house with a front porch and an enclosed veranda in a suburb of Hartford. She could stay there as long as she wanted as long as no one in the house used or sold illegal drugs. With a home for her children and an upcoming court date, Linda got ready to meet the judge with confidence. God was opening new doors, she said.

Linda went to probate court wearing her Salvation Army uniform. She was a changed woman and it showed in her smile and open evangelism. Her supporters filled the courtroom and there were others in the hallway.

Linda explained that she was no longer homeless and hadn't used drugs or had a drink for months. She had a place for the girls to sleep in her tiny two-bedroom apartment until the family's house in West Hartford was ready. She impressed the judge, who had rarely seen a woman with Linda's sordid history speak about change with such confidence.

Linda's motion for permanent visitation rights was grant-ed once she showed the judge certificates she had earned from Catholic Family Services, the Village of Families and Children and other commendations. She had completed a long-term treatment program, had recommendations from esteemed pro-fessionals and was employed with established community orga-nizations. She also told the judge that he need not worry about her parenting skills. She had taken a class for that, too.

Over the objections of attorneys for the state of Connect-icut's child protection agency, Linda's request for custody was also placed on the fast track.

"Thank you, Jesus," a woman from the audience yelled out. "You about to get yo' kids back, Linda."

The outburst was unnerving for the court. But almost ev-eryone in the courtroom rejoiced for Linda. The judge was most impressed by Linda's story about receiving housing from the Quakers, who owned the home. She said that if the family moved there she would have a greater shot of making sure her daugh-ters would receive a good education and would not be exposed to the lifestyle that she had led before she went into treatment.

Linda left the courtroom that day hopeful that if she con-tinued down her new path in life, none of her youngest daugh-ters would be labeled as an addict or an AIDS patient. She couldn't say the same thing about her eldest daughter Tanya, who she knew had become a crack addict and was acting reck-lessly in the streets of Hartford. Her only hope was that Tanya had a nice place to live with Mrs. Banks, her children's father.

Linda didn't go straight home after the hearing. There was no time to celebrate. She had promised someone at the church that she would do some evangelism work. She took the bus to a local grocery store where she handed out literature and rang the Salvation Army's charity bell.

"Do you know Jesus?" she asked complete strangers. "He saved my life."

Many of the people outside the store brushed her off in the same way she had done when she was actively using drugs and alcohol. But their rejection did not defeat her. She was confident that she had planted a seed that one day might take root.

Later that evening when Tasha, Nicole and Samantha came for a visit, she cooked them her famous fried chicken and gave them each a new pair of pajamas. The girls were puzzled because they hadn't spent the night with their mother for nearly a year. She was sober the entire weekend, and they didn't know how to respond to the changes they saw in her.

"Mommy, can we come back over?" Tasha asked.

"It won't be long before we'll all be back together," Linda told all of them.

Samantha, her youngest, was the happiest of the three girls. She wanted to get to know her mother, and cried when it was time to leave. She had longed for her mother's touch and was too young to remember the trauma that Linda had taken her through. She wondered if Tanya would also come home someday, because she had served as her surrogate mother when Linda wasn't able.

Linda went to work the following week with a new pep in

her step. She accepted more opportunities to speak to her peers about her newfound faith. She delivered her speeches about coping with the disease with wit and candor. Her personality made strangers comfortable, especially those who needed help and who had traveled down the same roads. They gravitated toward Linda. They didn't pity her because of all she had gone through. Her story was inspiring because she had been uplifted by her new relationship with God.

"AIDS saved my life," Linda told her audiences.

Almost everyone in the audience had never heard such proclamations about someone with the AIDS virus. So many others had proclaimed AIDS a death sentence and here Linda told them that she living with the virus when she had been killing herself before. She had played the role of a victim most of her life and had freed herself of such degrading thoughts. Her message of living with the disease attracted the attention of the media for a lot of reasons, but especially because Linda was refusing the medications that the doctors had prescribed.

She ignored the fact that her lymph nodes were growing on the side of her neck and her persistent cough showed that she was indeed experiencing the symptoms of AIDS. But Linda was adamant about refusing the new medicines her doctor prescribed. Her decision not to use the drugs was puzzling to most people in the HIV/AIDS community. But they couldn't help but notice that Linda looked healthy most of the time.

"God saved me before and he's not going to leave me now," she said.

The media in the Hartford area, her peers in the advocacy

community and so many others ignored Linda's symptoms in the same way she did, though they did pay attention to that cough. They had never heard anyone before call AIDS a lifesaver or a blessing. They didn't understand her faith but they felt drawn into her life story.

Linda looked forward to a bright future for herself and her family. But she wasn't prepared for the news that her oldest daughter Tanya had become hooked on crack cocaine in her twenties. She was pregnant for a third time and had also tested positive for the HIV virus.

Linda understood that Tanya had suffered for years as her oldest child because of her behavior. She understood that Tanya's drug use was due in part because of her need to escape memories of her parents' behavior. But Linda knew that if her daughter didn't change her life, she would turn her sons into orphans. If only Tanya could see the new Linda, and could forgive and forget the past. If only Tanya would stop running the streets, she could see how Linda had changed her life by trying to save addicts like herself who had also been diagnosed with the virus.

Linda wanted to save Tanya and other young women from the streets. Yet Linda knew deep down that Tanya was following in the path that she had traveled before she went into treatment.

"You stole my childhood," Tanya said once Linda confronted her.

"I know," Linda said. "But you can change if you want to. Do it for your boys, my grandchildren."

Linda was heartbroken when she heard through the family grapevine that one of her sisters had introduced Tanya to cocaine. The news tormented Linda and put her on the verge of a relapse. She felt angry enough to fight. She knew immediately that if she didn't collect herself, that she would lose the new life she had built for her daughters. She daydreamed about going to her sister's house and exposing her for smoking cocaine with Tanya. In the dream, she beat up her sister until she was bloody. But rather than going over to her sister's house, Linda kneeled beside her bed.

"Please God. Don't leave me now. Don't leave my daughters."

It was a simple prayer that relaxed Linda's nerves. The telephone rang. She was offered a chance to live in the five-bedroom house in West Hartford.

"Thank you, Jesus," Linda responded.

The telephone call was God's way of reminding Linda of the new rules she would have to follow if she wanted to live in the beautiful white house that had nice bedrooms, two porches and a front and back yard. The representative of the Quakers made Linda promise that no drugs, addicts or dealers could come into the house if she signed the lease. Otherwise, she would need to find another place to live, perhaps in one of Hartford's deteriorating housing projects, Stowe Village, Bellevue Square, Charter Oak or Nelton Court.

The chance to live in the beautiful single-family house on Maplewood Avenue in West Hartford reminded Linda of having a place of her own. She imagined painting the upstairs bathroom power blue with a shower curtain in a matching color. The older girls' rooms could be painted white, Samantha's room would be painted pink.

Those visions became a reality once Linda and three of her daughters moved in. She and her girls bonded as they decorated the house. The kitchen and pantry downstairs were Linda's favorite rooms. She had enough cabinet space to place her dishes and pots and pans. She hung the certificates she had earned in treatment in the pantry. The used furniture she received from donations looked great around the house. She knew that she could keep her promise to maintain a sober house as long as Alvin was in prison.

Samantha was too young to know how Linda acted when she was intoxicated. But Nicole knew. She recognized immediately that her mother had changed when she refused to give her money on demand and asked where she was going when she opened the front door.

"If you ask her for money you had to hear a whole story. 'I got to pay rent,'" Nicole said. "She is mean now."

But Nicole knew that she was safer at home with Linda than she had been when she stayed with her aunt. Her aunt's boyfriend had tried molesting her, and she knew the dangers of being away from her mother, who protected her even when she was strung out. The only other thing she hated was going to church all the time. Linda's new lifestyle was exposing both Nicole and Samantha to different things and different people. Nicole sometimes missed the old Linda, but they knew that the new Linda was better for them in the long run.

What Nicole disliked most about Linda's new notoriety was that her face was appearing on TV and in newspapers. Being a 16-year-old teenager at a predominantly white high school was difficult enough. She resented the fact that she didn't have any say over the work Linda was doing, especially after kids from her old neighborhood started teasing her.

"I was scared, but what is here is here. I give her credit. After she found out, she stopped using," Nicole said of her mother.

Then Alvin came home.

Linda couldn't say no to Alvin when she found out that he had pneumonia. She knew immediately that her husband was HIV positive, and she hoped that he would find his way into drug treatment. She tried nursing her husband back to health before she brought up the subject they were both avoiding. He had a fever and he needed to go to the doctor. She called the hospital, knowing that Alvin would try to fight her if she tried to make him go.

Alvin didn't fight Linda's decision to call an ambulance for two reasons. He was weak and he knew that the hospital was full of the narcotics he had craved since he was released from prison. When the ambulance arrived, the paramedics brought Alvin outside in a gurney. He was barely conscious and desperately needing antibiotics. His failing health worried Linda. She had never seen him that sick before. Was he going to die?

She didn't know the answer, but she prayed all through the day and night that Alvin would not die before he accepted Christ as his personal savior. His health was touch-and-go for more than a week.

Alvin had been sick for much longer than Linda knew. He hadn't sought treatment in prison because he didn't want to know what was wrong with him. He didn't have the strength for an HIV diagnosis. He knew the virus had really progressed to AIDS, the terminal illness that had killed thousands of men like him in America.

Linda worried and prayed enough for both of them.

Alvin was happy once he regained consciousness. He saw his family outside the prison bars that he had called home for so many years. He dreamed of getting better so he could party. He had heard that heroin was taking a backseat to eight-balls, a cocaine and heroin cocktail, and he wanted to try it. But he had to get better first.

In the meantime, Alvin was a cantankerous patient. He complained about the number of pillows on his bed. He hated the food and flipped the trays that were brought to his bed. He hated the way the nurses looked at him through cloth masks that covered much of their faces.

"They look like a bunch of damn monsters in the middle of the night," Alvin joked. "They woke me up and scared the shit out of me. Why everybody got on them damn masks. They think I'm goin' bite them or something. Broth and crackers? Who eats that shit!"

Alvin complained enough for his family to sneak in boxes of fried chicken for him to eat. His family watched his vulnerabilities with pity. He could barely chew. His mouth hurt from the sores and his bloated stomach ached when he swallowed. It took some time for the medicines to work on the numerous infections attacking Alvin's body.

The narcotics helped him sleep when he wasn't coughing, a symptom of full-blown AIDS. Other medical problems were worrying the doctors. They said Alvin's pancreas and liver were failing, and it showed in the yellowing of his eyes. The doctors wanted to do more tests, but Alvin wasn't ready to have surgery. If he could kick the pneumonia, he knew the staff would get tired of his mouthing off. They would send him home because he was a poor black man without insurance.

His plan worked. He woke up one morning and the tightness in his chest had loosened. He asked Linda to get his clothes, and she took him home. Alvin stayed in bed for another few weeks. His illness affected the entire family, who remembered that Alvin's cousin Logan had stayed in the basement before he died. Linda and the girls were afraid that Alvin would not survive, but they had forgotten that he was born tough and he would die tough. There were too many things for Alvin, who always had a mischievous nature, to get into before he passed away.

Alvin willed himself out of the bed one day and came back with a pocket full of cash, dope and liquor. He stayed high in the bedroom that he shared with Linda. She hated the sight of him because she knew that he'd try to drag her into the undertow of her previous addictions.

By allowing Alvin to live with her, Linda broke the house rules. He was an addict who brought drugs into the house. She had gotten so caught up in his physical condition that she didn't focus on her mistake until Nicole and Samantha found a hypodermic needle in the hamper. She got upset when they showed her the needle. The sight of it woke her up to the risk she was taking. She wanted to see Alvin through his recovery, but he wasn't trying. She was fed up.

Linda decided to divorce Alvin for the second time about the time he was arrested in Hartford on a misdemeanor charge in 1993. It was his thirty second arrest. The judge in the case had reviewed Alvin's criminal record before he was brought in for his arraignment. He had racked up a criminal record dating back to 1967. He had clever aliases: Alford Jordan, Alvin Barnes, Alwin Jordan, Eddie Lewis. Nothing but jail had stopped Alvin from drugging, stealing and driving stolen cars. Now, Alvin was heading back to prison. He had violated his parole.

Linda hated the fact that her husband was going back to prison. But she looked at it as a blessing. He was still alive.

She focused on her advocacy work and her new ministry of helping families living with HIV. She reached out to those who had not faced their demons and were still abusing drugs. Though her work was demanding, Linda didn't forget about her daughters. She attended counseling with Tasha, Nicole and Samantha, and took them to candlelight vigils, healing services and Narcotics Anonymous meetings. Nicole and Samantha became advocates in their own right. Nicole even worked as a babysitter at some of the meetings. Advocacy was not a vocation they chose and they didn't feel comfortable when Linda's photograph started appearing in newspapers.

She explained that she was not trying to embarrass the family, but she was working to save lives. On some weekends, Linda visited retreats in Litchfield County with other women in recovery. Nuns from the Sisters of Mercy sponsored Linda's expenses when she needed time away from her girls. The women she met on those retreats looked up to Linda. She had become their leader because she was real about her story and didn't hide the fact that she was still an addict. Many of the women who had kicked their habits had done so though methadone clinics. They were also HIV positive and were using the new medications to slow down their infections. Linda refused to take the drugs. If God had saved her from all she had gone through, He would keep her from dying of AIDS.

Linda and the others, including Danielle Warren-Diaz, learned about the art of meditation at the retreats. They gave each other makeovers and learned how to have safe sex. These kinds of workshops were new to Linda and the other women, who needed that kind of education to feel comfortable about living with HIV. The virus hadn't stolen their womanhood, Linda thought, as she walked the grounds with the other women in the group. They bonded as women in recovery.

At another retreat sponsored by Father Jerome Massameno of St. Patrick-St. Anthony's Catholic Church, the women were given their first full body massages. The relief they felt showed each of the women that they could relieve stress without using drugs. Each of them in their own way accepted themselves and each other. They would be friends for life.

One woman in the group learned she was HIV positive when she had a baby. She had known Linda and Alvin from the days when they got high together. The woman was in distress after the retreat. Her husband had passed away, leaving her with a sick baby boy. She was ready to jump off a bridge after her husband's funeral and was wandering aimlessly until she walked into a meeting at the Metropolitan A.M.E. Zion Church on Main Street. She was angry at her husband and at the disease that killed him.

Linda was her shepherd that day, taking the woman's hand and leading her out of the meeting. She listened more than she talked, and they parted knowing that they would always be sisters in the struggle. She was still alive, Linda told her. She had a baby to take care of.

Experiences like that kept Linda alive. So many women in Hartford and at meetings she attended across the country looked at Linda as a mentor. She was someone who kept it real. She was the leader of a group of seven women with children who were infected by the virus. They had all latched on to the notion that they could live. God had made it possible for Linda and all of them.

One woman stood out in the group. She had loved a man who intentionally infected her with the virus. The woman's story shocked the group. Many of the women were upset by her stupidity. But Linda stood up for the woman.

"We all got the virus," Linda said. "What does it matter how we got it? We can't give it back. All we can do now is live and help others."

Her words rang true. Now, it was time for her to put her face and the faces of her family on AIDS prevention posters. She had seen posters at different conferences and it puzzled her why no one who looked like her had ever posed for a picture. When she approached Darrell Decker, who was spearheading an AIDS prevention campaign, he agreed that if African-Americans were going to accept that the virus was spreading in their community, they'd have to see someone like Linda. He had heard her speak and liked her because her personality made her approachable to her audiences.

Linda's face became a symbol for a movement that was missing images of black AIDS activists. More than 30,000 posters of Linda and her family are still circulating the globe.

EPILOGUE | TWILIGHT

SILENCE TURNED INTO WHISPERS each time Linda stood before a new group and announced that she was HIV positive. That kind of honesty about her condition was unheard of in the latter part of the 20th century. The cloud of shame that Linda felt most of her life had lifted. African-Americans across the country were in denial, believing that their HIV status was a death sentence. Telling her story became easy.

Linda told her story not just to peers in confidential settings, but also to TV and newspaper reporters and at candlelight vigils. Her honesty shocked her family and all of Hartford. But her words became a catalyst for other women who had been afraid to talk about their HIV status.

Linda honed her public speaking skills and it showed. Religious leaders, the Urban League of Greater Hartford and Interfaith AIDS support groups invited her to continue telling her story. Her message hit the national scene as she traveled to AIDS conferences, was photographed for LIFE magazine, and continued delivering her message of hope despite her troubles at home. Alvin returned home from prison in 1996 and continued using dope. Her oldest daughter Tanya contracted the virus that causes AIDS from her boyfriend.

Linda, a well-known AIDS educator, activist and group leader, grieved for Alvin when he died in January 1996. But she found it even more difficult to overcome Tanya's death in May 2004. Both died of AIDS-related illnesses.

The AIDS virus, and the grief following the loss of loved ones, finally overcame her. She retired to her bed once she "graduated" from HIV to an AIDS diagnosis. She had lost her sight and found it difficult to walk. She quietly disappeared from the limelight and got ready to go to God. Barbara, her visiting nurse, said Linda never lost her faith. Late into the night, when Samantha, Tasha and their children were asleep, Barbara said, she sat at Linda's bedside and Linda would be whispering the 23rd Psalm.

Her message of living with AIDS survived her death on May 1, 2006. Linda Jordan died surrounded by her father Daddy Harry, children and grandchildren. Tasha, Nicole and Samantha survive their mother; all are single mothers working low-paying jobs.

Nearly five hundred people attended Linda's funeral in the Salvation Army's gymnasium on Barbour Street in Hartford's North End. It was a joyous celebration where she was remembered as a pioneer in the HIV/AIDS and substance abuse community. She was a woman who turned a crooked road straight and embraced the new life that God gave her almost twenty years.

DISCUSSION TIPS FOR "CROOKED ROAD STRAIGHT"

AUTHOR TINA A. BROWN addresses in "Crooked Road Straight: The Awakening of AIDS Activist Linda Jordan" some critical issues facing those at risk of contracting HIV/AIDS. Her book takes readers down Linda Jordan's harrowing journey to recovery and action.

As facilitators of support groups across the country prepare to hold meaningful discussions, consider addressing the following questions in your group:

1. Could you relate to what Linda Jordan faced as a child? What problems in her family structure directed her down the crooked path? Formulate questions about how Linda dealt with hurtful situations in her life.
2. Did you have strong reactions to the characters? Which character produced the strongest reaction? Why?
3. Describe Linda's relationship with Alvin? Why do you think she stayed with him? How did this relationship shape Linda's addiction and life choices?
4. How did Linda's dependence on government support shape her life story?
5. Describe Linda's relationship with her children.
6. What role did Linda's religious conversion play in her story?
7. What courageous steps did Linda take?
8. What was the author's vision? Why did she write the book? Will this book benefit people at risk of contracting HIV/AIDS and those already infected?
9. Describe the author's style and voice?
10. Do the overall themes of this book compel you to take action? If so, how?